The Complete
Caravan Book

CONTENTS

Whether you are buying your first caravan, or simply want to be more adventurous with your tourer, *The Complete Caravan Book* tells you everything that you need to know, from choosing a caravan, to getting ready for your holiday and caravan maintenance.

Checking your weight distribution before setting off ▶

▲ Getting your water supply into the caravan

Connecting up to the site's mains electricity ▶

▼ Going through your pre-journey checks

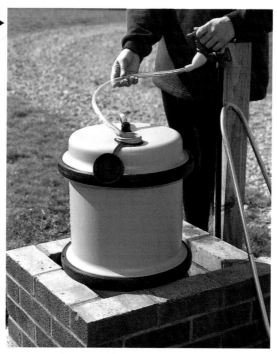

▲ Choosing essential accessories such as towing mirrors

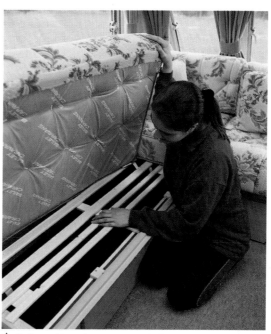

▲ Finding out how storage space works in your caravan

WRITTEN BY
Ally Watson

EDITOR
Ann Kay

ART DIRECTOR
Traci Rochester

PHOTOGRAPHY
Andrew Dee
and George Wright

ILLUSTRATIONS
Geoff Denney

MANAGING EDITOR
Felicity Jackson

PRODUCTION CONTROLLER
Louise McIntyre

Ally Watson has asserted her right to be identified as the author of this work.

First published 1997

© Haynes Publishing 1997

Published by:
Haynes Publishing
Sparkford, Nr Yeovil,
Somerset BA22 7JJ

British Library Cataloguing-in-Publication Data:
A catalogue record for this book is available from the British Library

ISBN 1 85960 123 5

Printed in Italy by
G. Canale & C. S.p.A. –
Borgaro Torinese (Turin)

Caravanning for all

The kind of caravan featured in this book is the rigid-sided trailer type, built on an axle and chassis for towing behind a vehicle and equipped with sleeping, cooking and washing facilities. The combination of a living unit and a powered unit that can move it goes back to 1914, when the first caravan built specifically to be towed behind a car was made.

Right: Early models were far more cumbersome than the tourers of today. It was also much more important that the appearance should be instantly familiar – the front door on this model looks just like the door of a 1930s suburban house!

Below: Caravanning continues to bring freedom, convenience and inexpensive holidaying to all kinds of people – and models are constantly improving.

The roots of the trailer caravan as we know it today lie in the mid-1820s, when large horse-drawn vehicles were built for travelling showmen. By the mid-1860s, trailer caravans had become popular with gypsies, who until this time had used tents and so, contrary to popular belief, were not responsible for the invention of the caravan.

'Gentlemen gypsies'

The first caravanners were the 'gentlemen gypsies' of the late 18th and early 19th century. Their palatial, horse-drawn caravans were weighed down with so many home comforts that they had to be towed by extremely strong horses. They were usually accompanied on their adventures by a footman, who would attend to their master's every need and sleep in a small compartment at the back of the caravan, or in a tent close by.

Caravanning gained in popularity throughout the 1930s and 1940s, when tourers resembled mobile cottages with their leaded windows and overhanging roof lines, and entered its boom time during the 1960s and 1970s.

Get up and go

Today's trailer caravan is a purpose-built leisure vehicle, designed to help you tour in total comfort. Once you arrive on a site you'll find that most caravan parks have been designed purely to provide a peaceful retreat. All the necessary things for everyday life are there – shower rooms, toilets, basic provisions, play areas for children and water and electricity supply points – so that you can spend your days just relaxing. Most people today have a car and use it a great deal for leisure pursuits, so a caravan is a natural progression from this.

Caravanning for all

Caravanning has got something for most people. Most sites are level so that pitching a caravan is simple, and walking is made as easy as possible for those who may have difficulties. Elderly caravanners can usually specify a pitch close to amenities to save on walking and flat, metalled site roads are often highly accessible to wheelchair users. Also, many parks now have at least a shower room with washbasin and toilet for people with

disabilities or those using wheelchairs. Perhaps the most important thing is that there's always someone around on site to lend a hand.

It's not just the sites that are easily accessible – the compact space of a caravan can be a great advantage for those with mobility problems. For people who want to use a wheelchair in their caravan, some dealerships can convert caravans to give wider door access, and lower furniture and fittings. Some companies that build by hand may be able to make design changes to suit particular needs at little extra charge.

The social side

Because there's such a sense of community on site, it's easy to make new friends quickly. You can also join various caravanning clubs, some of which are based on the make of your caravan (see caravanning magazines for details), and these can provide a valuable source of information, as well as enjoyable social events.

The major national clubs are the biggest and have a range of services, from arranging travel to providing insurance and breakdown and recovery services. They also have networks of sites which they either own, manage or recommend (which are usually of a very high standard) and produce a club magazine that is a useful source of suppliers, caravans for sale and other readers' experiences.

Above: Many parks are in beautiful settings, designed to provide as much tranquillity as possible.

The perfect base

Your caravan is not just something to be towed to a site and left there while you get on with your holiday. If you have hobbies that take you away from home, a caravan is extremely useful as a base camp. You'll always have somewhere warm and dry to come back to, where you can cook a hearty meal to set yourself up for the next day's exertions.

Close to the action

You can get close to all kinds of popular activities with a caravan. Events such as motor-racing, music festivals, country shows and fairs often have an area where caravans can pitch – and these are frequently held in places where there are no hotels. A trailer caravan isn't just somewhere to cook, sleep, store your clothes, wash and eat. It's also somewhere warm and comfortable to unwind and socialize at the end of the day without the trouble of having to find a special place to go.

Active holidays

There is no end to the range of activities that a caravan can make more enjoyable. Awning annexes are ideal for keeping bikes out of the rain, while racks fitted to your car or inside/outside your caravan make it easy to take the whole family's bikes with you on holiday.

Because most caravans are fully insulated, they are perfect as a base for winter sports. Look for a caravan with a 'wet' locker at the front. This is a waterproofed locker with a lockable door that runs the width of the caravan – perfect for storing skis, poles, damp ski clothing and snowboards. A wet locker is also useful for outdoor pursuits such as fishing, walking, horseriding or boating.

If they don't enjoy walking already, many caravanners are quickly converted. Whether it's a gentle stroll around the perimeter of the park or a lengthy hike across rough terrain, a caravan places you in the countryside, close to trails, paths and walkways. Site receptions often keep comprehensive details of good walks to be had nearby.

Many larger sites have tennis courts, swimming pools – even gym facilities. Some bigger parks have mountain bike hire, pony trekking, coarse fishing or even their own on-site stretch of stream.

Leisurely pursuits

Don't, however, think that you have to be active and outgoing to go caravanning – simply enjoying the countryside and more leisurely pursuits is an excellent reason to buy a touring caravan. Gentle activities such as photography and bird- and wildlife-watching are all possible in and around a park – a caravan makes a perfect 'hide' and sites are usually teeming with wildlife, from squirrels to birds, deer and rabbits. For those with children, this is the perfect place for them to play and make friends – in a safe area where they are under the watchful eye of fellow caravanners.

Touring
CARAVANS

A touring caravan is a ticket to holiday freedom. You can get away when you like, and go almost anywhere you want. While hotel-based holidays can be expensive, and self-catering accommodation ties you to one area, a tourer gives you the option of a different destination every time you set out. If you don't like it when you get there, you can move on. You might also be surprised at just how comfortable and convenient even basic tourers can be – a real home on wheels.

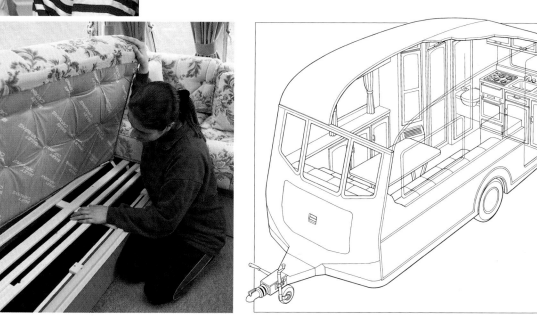

Chapter 1 takes you right inside your tourer – from what to expect in your living space to basic construction

Construction

All European caravans are manufactured to standards governing safety and quality in both materials and workmanship. They are designed for all-year-round use, to be cool in the summer and warm during winter. The majority are made on factory production lines, although there are manufacturers who build caravans by hand, using traditional methods.

HOW IS IT MADE?

● Most caravans are built on an **ASSEMBLY LINE**, just like cars, except that the process is far less automated

1. THE CARAVAN STARTS LIFE at one end of the factory, as a chassis and floor, before working its way down the 'line', having the other parts added. Any fitted carpet is also put in at this stage

2. WIRES AND PIPES to carry electricity, gas and water are now put in, ready to be connected to equipment. Key appliances such as the space heater and fridge are added

3. FURNITURE and dividing partitions go on next and, depending on their size and shape, are fixed to either the floor or the sides. Unlike car assembly, making a caravan is still fairly labour-intensive – joiners are often employed to make the furniture, for example

4. THE SIDES, which will have been made separately, are fixed to the floor and to the back of the furniture. Roof lockers will already have been fixed to the sides and there will be holes for windows, doors and so on

5. THE ROOF goes on and the front and back GRP or plastic panels are fixed in place. Lastly, the windows, door, vents and locker doors are added

6. Before THE CARAVAN LEAVES THE FACTORY, all systems are tested and the caravan is passed for sale

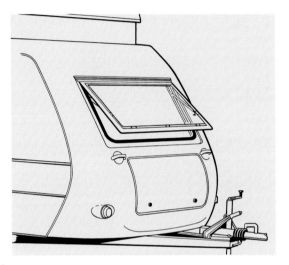

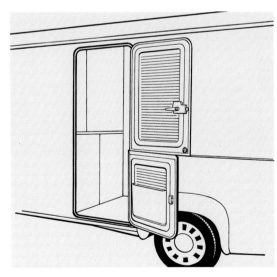

Illustrations on this page: Caravan windows are double-glazed and doors are commonly made in a stable-door style. Both the floor and sides are insulated.

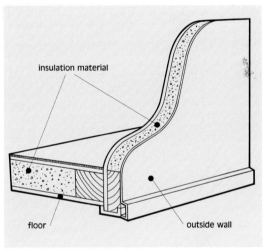

insulation material

floor

outside wall

Windows and doors

Windows are double-glazed units made of acrylic, usually bought in from specialist makers. The majority are frameless and, when fastened, fit snugly against a rubber strip around the edge of the window. Traditional 'stable' doors have top halves that open independently.

Sides and floors

These are constructed on the sandwich principle. In the case of the caravan's sides, the 'bread' is the interior panel on one side and the exterior panel — with the caravan's aluminium skin on it — on the other. The 'filling' is insulation. The floor, which is basically insulation material sandwiched between wood, is bolted to the chassis.

Roofs

The roof framework is usually added in the final stages. If the caravan roof is flat, the aluminium skin will be rolled onto it and gently hammered over at the edges (to be sealed and disguised later by trim). In the case of a 'boat' or 'V' roof, the skin is in two halves, with a seam down the middle. Some roofs are GRP (Glass-fibre Reinforced Plastic) mouldings.

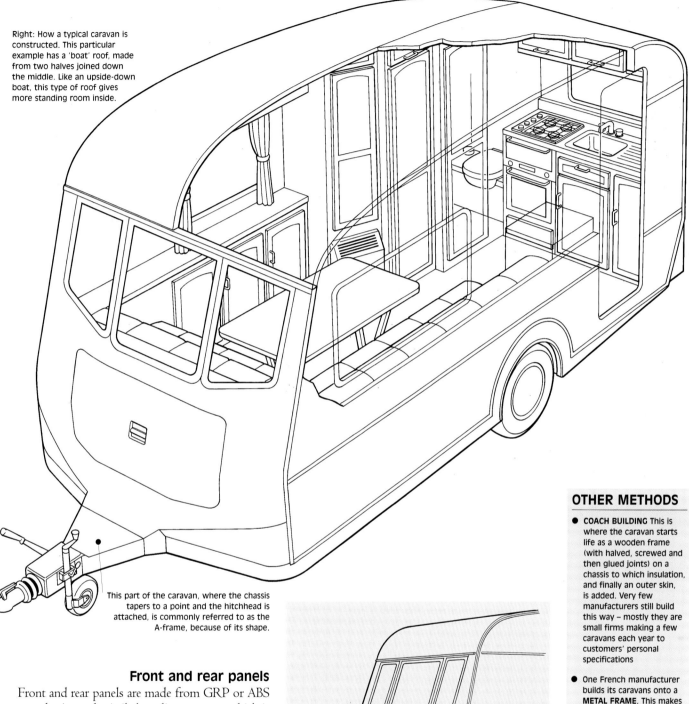

Right: How a typical caravan is constructed. This particular example has a 'boat' roof, made from two halves joined down the middle. Like an upside-down boat, this type of roof gives more standing room inside.

This part of the caravan, where the chassis tapers to a point and the hitchhead is attached, is commonly referred to as the A-frame, because of its shape.

Front and rear panels

Front and rear panels are made from GRP or ABS plastic acrylonitrile butadiene-styrene, which is moulded into streamlined shapes and then used to cap the front and rear of the caravan. Holes positioned to accommodate windows, doors and so on mean that each manufacturer's panels have to be tailor-made.

Right: The gas locker door is in the front panel. This locker is basically the space between the outer front panel and the inside front wall.

OTHER METHODS

● **COACH BUILDING** This is where the caravan starts life as a wooden frame (with halved, screwed and then glued joints) on a chassis to which insulation, and finally an outer skin, is added. Very few manufacturers still build this way – mostly they are small firms making a few caravans each year to customers' personal specifications

● One French manufacturer builds its caravans onto a **METAL FRAME**. This makes even its smallest models heavy, but much sturdier – especially in the event of an accident

● **ALL-GRP CARAVANS** are rare because of the relatively high production costs and the extra weight that this material adds. Their main advantages are that they are easily repaired and reasonably tough

The chassis

The chassis is the most important part of any trailer caravan. This is the base onto which the caravan is built and it provides all the parts that a caravan needs to perform its touring duties – wheels, brakes, a coupling to attach it to the car, a safety device if it breaks free while you're towing and steadying devices to stop it rocking about when it's unhitched on site.

CHASSIS FACTS

- The chassis and axle are the **LOAD-BEARING** parts of the caravan

- Most European caravans are now built on chassis made by a **GERMAN COMPANY**, Al-Ko Kober

- Some manufacturers build **THEIR OWN CHASSIS**

- You can tell the **AGE OF A CARAVAN** by the combination of numbers/letters on the chassis plate. Each year of manufacture has a different code

- Your **CARAVAN HANDBOOK** will tell you which chassis your caravan is built on

- **NEVER DRILL** a galvanized chassis without consulting the manufacturer – you could weaken it or invalidate your warranty

- Chassis are **MADE OF** aluminium (less common today) or steel

- **MODERN CHASSIS** are in the shape of an 'A', with tapering arms at each side

Coupling or hitchhead

This is the part of the chassis that 'hitches' – joins – the car to the caravan. The cup goes over the top of the car's towball and a locking device fits under the lower half. The handle on top of the hitchhead must be lifted when hitching and unhitching to free the locking device.

Handbrake

When the caravan is not hitched to the car, its handbrake must always be fully engaged. Only when the caravan is hitched up, and all the connections have been made between car and caravan, should the handbrake be taken off.

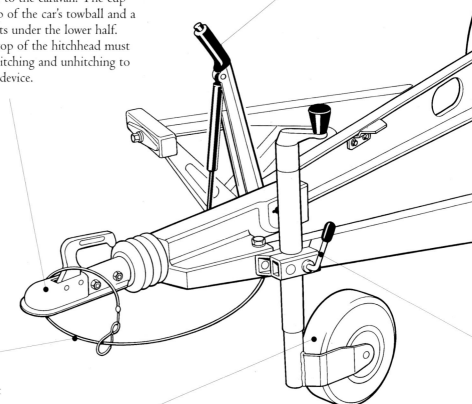

Breakaway cable

A safety device with a built-in weak spot. It is fixed to the towbar in such a way that, should the hitchhead or towball fail, it will first pull on the caravan's handbrake – bringing it to a standstill – and then snap. This stops a 'runaway' caravan causing havoc with other traffic.

Jockey wheel

A small wheel on a telescopic shaft that is wound down to hold the nose of the caravan level when it is not hitched to a car. Without its jockey wheel down, an unhitched caravan will plunge nose-down to the ground. When towing, the jockey wheel is wound up out of the way.

Axle

Caravan suspension is quite different to that found in cars. An inner 'tube' is offset at a 45-degree angle to an outer 'tube' and the spaces in between are filled with lengths of rubber. The wheel is connected to this system by a trailing arm. When the wheel moves up and down, the rubber is compressed and then released.

Corner steady

These metal 'legs' are wound down using the specially designed handle (or corner steady winder), which fits over a central, threaded rod. They are designed to 'steady' the caravan so that it doesn't rock about when it's unhitched and you're inside. They must never be used to level the caravan on site as this can twist the chassis.

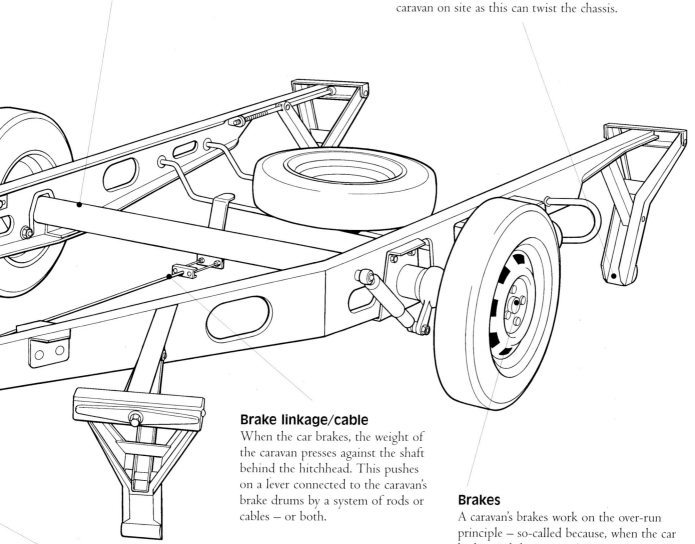

Brake linkage/cable

When the car brakes, the weight of the caravan presses against the shaft behind the hitchhead. This pushes on a lever connected to the caravan's brake drums by a system of rods or cables – or both.

Brakes

A caravan's brakes work on the over-run principle – so-called because, when the car brakes and the caravan 'over-runs' towards the car, the brakes are applied. Once the car moves off again, the brakes are released. This system only works if the caravan wheels are moving forwards; when they rotate the other way, the brakes disengage.

Jockey wheel clamp

This small handle is turned two or three times to clamp the wheel into position so that it cannot move about. Then the jockey wheel can be wound either up or down as desired.

Your living space

Among the first things you'll be looking at in any caravan are its storage potential and its living area. You'll always take more than you need on holiday, so you want good storage areas of different shapes and sizes. And a main living area with all the luxuries of a comfortable lounge is very important, especially if you are planning long trips.

Above: The front locker is a really useful piece of furniture. As well as storing things inside, you could put your TV on here, or eat light snacks off the fold- or slide-out top shelf that many models have.

Storage space

Families on holiday need lots of storage space for clothes. Small, individual lockers at head height are great for T-shirts and jumpers. As well as hanging space, a caravan wardrobe usually has vertical, shelved storage for shirts, shoes, socks and so on.

Multi-purpose furniture

Almost every piece of furniture in the caravan doubles up as something else. The most obvious example is seating that turns into beds (see below). Low-level cupboards between the front seats often change into coffee tables with the pull of a flap; sink-covers flip over the edge of the kitchen unit to become an extra work-surface area; and sectioned wooden doors pull out to become partitions between sleeping areas.

Seating

As well as being a comfortable place for lounging during the day or evening, the seats in a caravan double as beds for night-time.

Right: Not only does caravan seating convert into beds, it also conceals a huge storage area where you can keep all your bedding. Just lift the lid or pull back the slats for access.

Above: Roof lockers have special travel catches that resist weight – staying firmly closed when you are on the move.

14

Above: There are usually two tables in a family caravan. One, like the table shown here, commonly stands on a pedestal leg or has a support leg and clips to the wall. The other table is freestanding and, when you buy your caravan, is found stowed away flat against a wall.

SAVING SPACE

Things have a dual purpose in caravans to save on the two vital commodities – space and weight. In an area that can be as small as 3m and as 'large' as 6m, space is very precious. Adding too much weight in the form of furniture and fittings would mean that the average family car would be less likely to be able to tow the caravan.

Left: The front seating area is often called the 'main' area of the caravan because this is where most families eat and the parents sleep. In a caravan designed to sleep two people, it is the only seating area.

Cooking and washing

What kinds of facilities do you want in your caravan? One of the advantages of caravanning over staying in hotels is that you can cook for yourself. You can opt for just a basic hob top, or choose a complete oven with grill. Likewise, decide whether you want to be able to shower in your caravan or are happy to use the on-site facilities.

Washing facilities

All commercial sites have toilets and showers. If you intend staying on farm or forest sites with very basic facilities (if any), then you will probably want hot water to the kitchen and washroom, plus a toilet.

Ventilation

Caravans are designed for easy ventilation. Windows open until horizontal and there are roof lights in the ceiling with 'pop-up' covers. The more expensive caravans often have extractor fans over their hobs.

Above: This wash-basin mixer tap has a dual role. If you pull it out of its mounting and fix it to the bracket on the washroom wall, it instantly becomes a shower head.

Above: Some caravans have fixed corner wash-basins; others save space by using a 'tip-up' sink, shown here. This is tipped up after use to empty water out through pipes at the back. It folds flat against the vanity unit when not in use.

Above: It is only fairly recently that chemical toilets became a standard fixture. If you are buying secondhand, you may have to fit your own.

Cooking

All caravans have at least a hob with burners on it. More sophisticated tourers have a hob plus an oven and grill. These are always fuelled by gas, as it would take too much power to use electricity.

Food preparation

The amount of space given over to preparing food varies. All tourers have a space near the sink; some have a kitchen area that extends right across the end wall or units with pull- or fold-out work surfaces.

Kitchen storage

Roof lockers and kitchen cupboards give a variety of food storage areas. Other features may include pull-out cupboards with wire baskets in them for storing vegetables, and lipped cupboard shelves that will hold in foodstuffs securely. There is usually a large cupboard underneath the oven unit for storing pans. Plates, cups and bowls have their own rack in one of the overhead lockers. As caravans have fridges, it's possible to store and cook perishables.

Above: In this kitchen, a flap folds down over the draining area to form food preparation/serving space. A full oven (big enough to cook a family meal), with a grill and piezo ignition hob, is common.

Above: This kitchen drawer has an integral cutlery holder and a large storage cupboard below it. Plates are stowed securely in a special rack. Note the roof-light, for ventilation, in the ceiling. The one shown here has a screen underneath that keeps insects out when the roof-light is open.

Left: The caravan kitchen is well-equipped and pleasant to work in – there's always a window for a view of the outside world.

Electricity supply

In order to power the equipment fitted into it, every modern caravan has an integral electricity system. All modern tourers have at least a low-voltage supply from a 12V on-board leisure battery. It is increasingly common for this to be supplemented by power from an on-site mains supply, by simply connecting the caravan to it with a special lead.

POWER POINTS

- Site mains supplies have a **MAXIMUM TOTAL AMPERAGE** that you can use at any one time. This can vary within the same country

- **CALCULATE HOW MUCH POWER** is drawn by each item you will use on mains electricity (this is usually detailed on product packaging or literature). That way, you won't exceed the site's amp allowance, possibly tripping out everyone else!

- You will need to know **HOW MANY WATTS** there are in different amperages, so here is a handy reference table (W = V x A):

2 amps	=	400 watts
4A	=	800W
6A	=	1200W
8A .	=	1600W
10A	=	2000W
16A	=	3000W

Battery box

This is the storage space where the caravan's 12V leisure battery is kept. The terminals to connect the battery to the 12V system are in here. If your caravan has mains electrics, the inlet for the mains connection cable may also be in here.

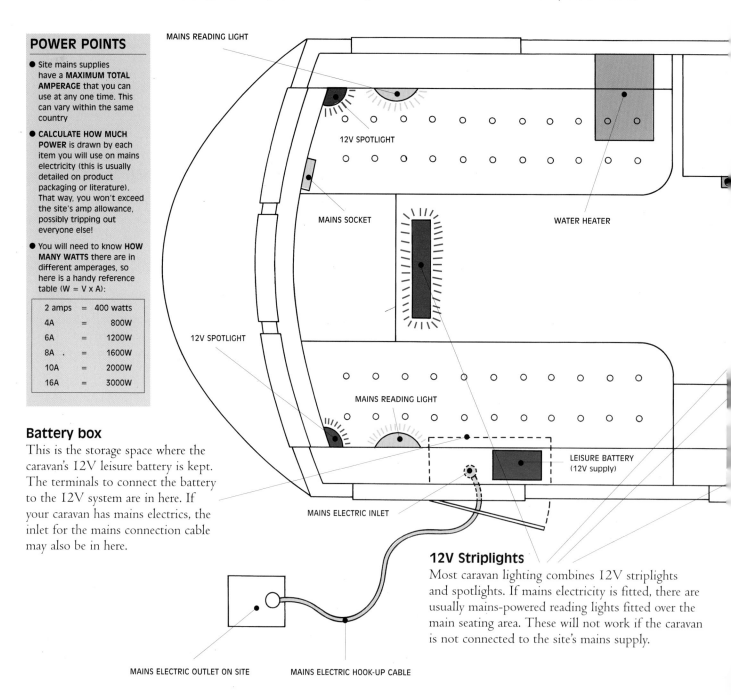

MAINS READING LIGHT

12V SPOTLIGHT

MAINS SOCKET

WATER HEATER

12V SPOTLIGHT

MAINS READING LIGHT

LEISURE BATTERY (12V supply)

MAINS ELECTRIC INLET

MAINS ELECTRIC OUTLET ON SITE

MAINS ELECTRIC HOOK-UP CABLE

12V Striplights

Most caravan lighting combines 12V striplights and spotlights. If mains electricity is fitted, there are usually mains-powered reading lights fitted over the main seating area. These will not work if the caravan is not connected to the site's mains supply.

Spark ignition for space heater

Although caravan space heaters work off gas, any electronic ignition is provided by a 12V (battery) electricity supply if it is not provided by piezo crystal igniter. If the heater has a fan, with ducts through which warm air is distributed around the caravan, then this can often be worked from mains or 12V, too. The controls for this are frequently positioned next to the control panel, for neatness.

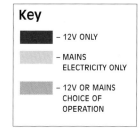

Key

■ – 12V ONLY

▨ – MAINS ELECTRICITY ONLY

▨ – 12V OR MAINS CHOICE OF OPERATION

⚠ WHAT POWERS WHAT?

- **MAINS ELECTRICITY** allows many domestic electrical items to be used in the caravan, such as toasters and TVs, hair-dryers and some fan-heaters

- **THE 12V BATTERY SUPPLY** is used to power things like striplights, the electric flush operation of some toilets, the water pump and other items that don't draw too much power

- There is also **SOME CROSS-OVER** between the two systems, even though they are entirely separate – for example, the fridge can be used on either 12V or mains

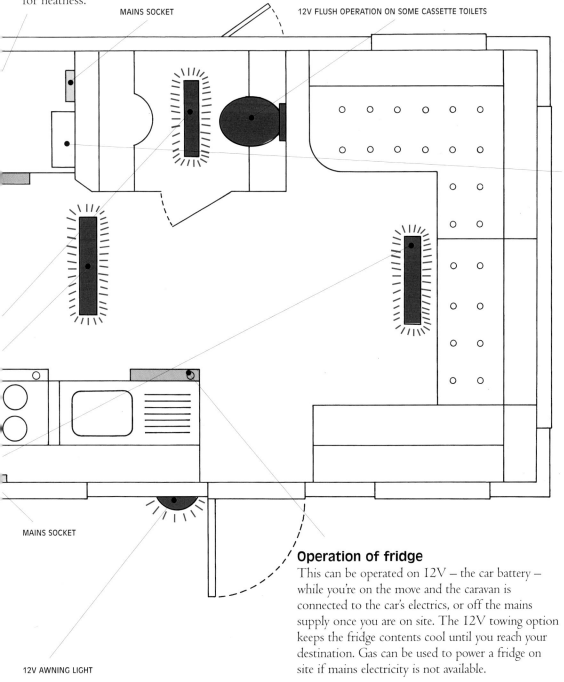

MAINS SOCKET

12V FLUSH OPERATION ON SOME CASSETTE TOILETS

MAINS SOCKET

12V AWNING LIGHT

Control panel for all electrics

This is where all the switches and fuses are for the 12V battery supply. The principal rocker switch, labelled 'car', 'off' and 'caravan', allows control of the power supply. Switch to 'car' to perform tasks like battery charging from the car in emergencies. Switch to 'caravan' when you are on site and want to use the 12V supply. Some manufacturers neaten things up by putting the controls for 12V/mains appliances here, too. The Residual Current Device (which disconnects the electricity supply in case of an accident) for the mains supply will be tucked away elsewhere in the caravan – sometimes at the bottom of the wardrobe.

Operation of fridge

This can be operated on 12V – the car battery – while you're on the move and the caravan is connected to the car's electrics, or off the mains supply once you are on site. The 12V towing option keeps the fridge contents cool until you reach your destination. Gas can be used to power a fridge on site if mains electricity is not available.

Gas system

All caravans are equipped to use LPG (liquefied petroleum gas). With your caravan's gas supply connected up, all is not lost if the caravan battery goes flat and you're on a site with no mains hook-ups. You'll still be able to heat water, cook and run your space heater. Gas cylinders are carried on-board in a special locker at the front or side of the caravan.

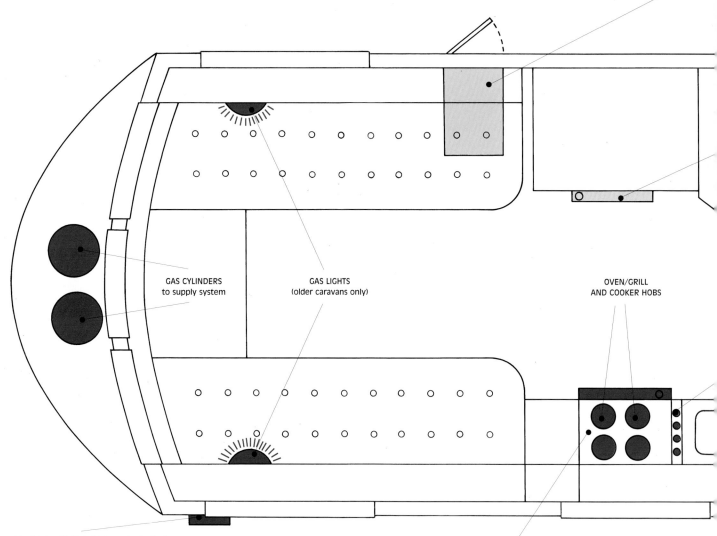

GAS CYLINDERS
to supply system

GAS LIGHTS
(older caravans only)

OVEN/GRILL
AND COOKER HOBS

External barbecue point

In the last few years, some manufacturers have started fitting external barbecue points to their caravans. Gas-fired barbecues can then simply be 'plugged' into the caravan's system, without the need to take a cylinder out of the gas locker in order to connect it to the barbecue.

Cooking

A gas hob, oven and grill make fast, easy work of cooking in a caravan. Many burners have piezo ignition and all new caravans are fitted with flame-failure devices for safety. This is because hobs are often close to caravan doors, where draughts may blow out the flames.

Water heater

A tank of water can be heated in around 20 minutes. This can then be drawn into the washroom basin or shower or the kitchen sink. As a wise economy measure, use gas to heat up the water initially and then, if necessary, keep the temperature going during the day with mains electricity.

Space heater

The standard caravan space heater is now the flued variety. Air is drawn in from outside and mixed with gas from the caravan's supply. The mixture is then burned so that warmed air passes through a type of radiator before leaving the caravan via a flue. This ensures that no gas or combustion products remain inside the tourer and cuts down condensation.

GAS FACTS

- Gas **DOES NOT FLOW DIRECTLY** from the cylinder to the appliance. Isolator taps for each appliance are commonly found in the kitchen area, usually under the sink

- **A FLEXIBLE HOSE** from your caravan's gas system is found in the gas locker. A regulator (to regulate the flow of gas from the cylinder) is fitted to the end of this and then on to the cylinder itself

- **THE SIZE** of gas cylinders varies from country to country, although Camping Gaz is sold all over Europe

- When your **CYLINDER IS EMPTY**, simply 'exchange' it by taking the empty to a supplier and purchasing more gas. Look out for signs offering 'gas exchange' at sites and petrol stations

- **GAS CAN FREEZE** in winter. Use Butane (blue cylinder) during warm months as it freezes at less than 0 °C. For winter use, change to Propane (red cylinder), which remains liquefied up to -40 °C

- **NEVER BLOCK** the in-built means of gas escape – the wall vents and gas 'drop holes' in the floor (gas is heavier than air). They prevent a harmful build-up of fumes

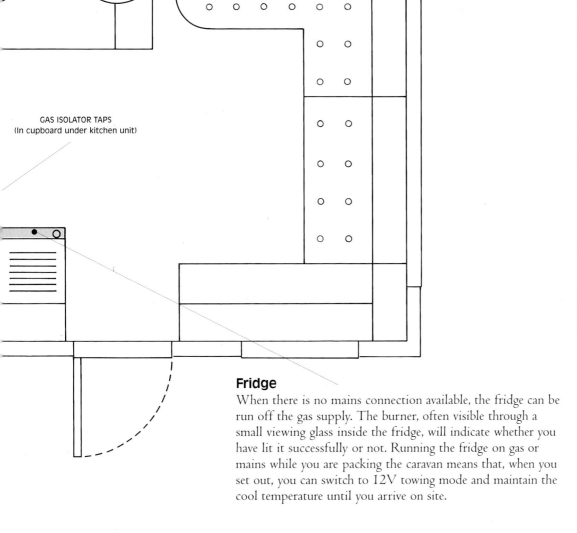

GAS ISOLATOR TAPS
(In cupboard under kitchen unit)

Key

■ – OPERATED BY GAS ONLY

▨ – OPERATED BY GAS OR ELECTRICITY

Fridge

When there is no mains connection available, the fridge can be run off the gas supply. The burner, often visible through a small viewing glass inside the fridge, will indicate whether you have lit it successfully or not. Running the fridge on gas or mains while you are packing the caravan means that, when you set out, you can switch to 12V towing mode and maintain the cool temperature until you arrive on site.

CHAPTER 2

Choosing a CARAVAN

Whether you'll be buying a new tourer or a used one, it's important to establish what type of caravan will suit your holiday needs best. How often will you use it? Who will be caravanning with you? What sort of cooking and sleeping arrangements would you like? You also need to know what to look for in a good caravan and what to avoid. Armed with this information, you'll find it much easier to look for the right caravan – at the right price.

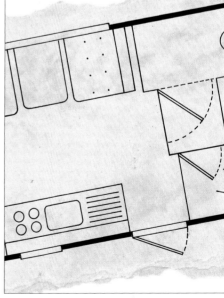

Take time over assessing the best fittings and layout for your needs

Family layouts

There are no set rules about where a caravan's fixtures and fittings go. Some items are put in certain locations for practical reasons or to comply with safety regulations. Beyond this, it is up to each manufacturer to decide how the rest of the caravan looks. There are over 50 popular caravan layouts – the ones shown here are just a few of those suitable for families.

WHAT TO LOOK FOR

- **WOODEN PARTITIONS** between sleeping areas offer better sound-proofing than the curtains that are sometimes fitted, so look out for this if you have young children

- What are the **AGES AND WEIGHTS** of those who will have to sleep in bunks? The maximum age/weight for which the bunk is designed will be supplied.

- **LARGE WINDOWS** across the back of the caravan may be dangerous if you have small children sleeping in bunks there – they could roll over and fall out of the caravan

- Most bunks have small **GUARDS** to stop children falling out of bed and onto the caravan floor. Bunk nets that cover the whole of the bunk side are available from caravan accessory shops

READING THE CODES

When you start to look at caravans you will notice that, as well as a model name, the majority also have a series of numbers and letters. For example, in a 500/5 model, the 500 usually denotes the interior body length in centimetres and 5 denotes the number of berths or beds.

You may also see the letters CK (central kitchen), EK (end kitchen), CT (central toilet) and ET (end toilet). The letters SE, GT, GTX and GTS are similar to those letters used to describe the levels of luxury, trim or body style of cars. On a caravan, they simply indicate a more sophisticated model.

End washrooms

In larger tourers, or those with a second dinette at the side of the caravan, an 'end washroom' arrangement is possible. This means that, instead of having all the washing facilities in one compact washroom, they are placed in a strip that runs right across the back of the caravan. You may have a separate shower compartment on one side and a toilet and wash-basin on the other, with a dressing area in between. Other end washroom layouts have a toilet and shower on one side, a wardrobe on the other and a vanity unit with wash-basin against the back wall of the caravan.

Below: This four-berth has a front double plus a single bed to the side with a bunk above.

Below: A layout with a permanently fixed double bed.

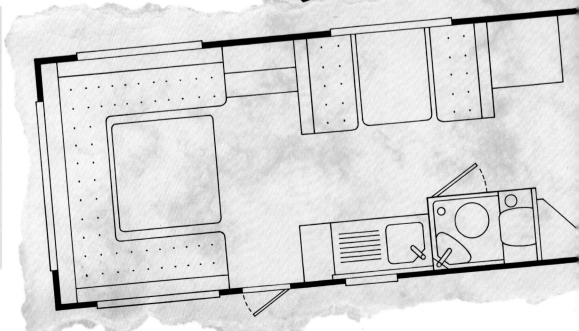

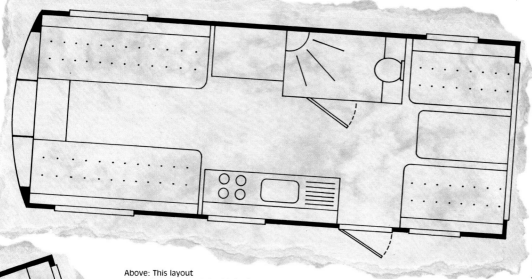

Fixed beds

If you plan to spend a lot of time touring, then a layout with fixed beds may be useful. Instead of converting your seating area to beds every night and then back to seats every morning, fixed beds are just like your beds at home. They have a mattress and headboard and offer plenty of bedding storage underneath. Partition doors are usually fitted to close this sleeping area off from the rest of the van during the day or when you have guests.

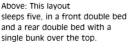

Above: This layout sleeps five, in a front double bed and a rear double bed with a single bunk over the top.

Below: An L-shaped front seating area features in this four-berth.

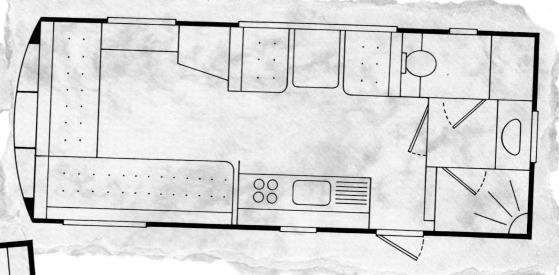

Double dinettes

This layout can sleep four, five or even six people. The dinette at the front of the caravan converts to a double bed and is usually used by the adults. The second dinette at the back or side of the caravan may then convert to a smaller double bed (for two small children or another couple), with one or even two single bunks over the top (sleeping up to two more children or teenagers).

L-shaped seating

This type of seating has become very fashionable over the last few years. It is taking the place of the once-standard facing seats, giving lots of leg-room and a more informal, sociable way of seating guests. One disadvantage of this type of seating in the main area is that, because the cushions wrap all the way around the front of the caravan, it isn't possible for the manufacturers to fit a central chest of drawers/occasional table here, which many caravanners find extremely handy.

Just for two

The choice is vast if there's just two of you caravanning. You can select from layouts designed specifically to accommodate couples or, if you like plenty of room, choose a family berth layout and enjoy all the extra space this gives you. Because there are fewer beds to fit in, caravan designers can be rather more imaginative with two-berth layouts.

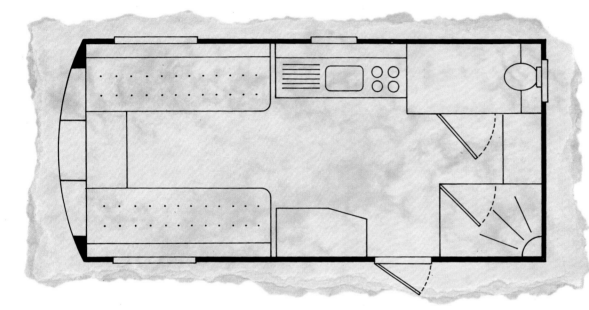

Front dinette

The front dinette in a two-berth caravan tends to be bigger than its family berth counterpart, so it's possible to keep the seats (if they are in the traditional parallel arrangement) as two full-length singles — rather than a double — if desired.

Left: This washroom has separate shower and toilet compartments, with a wardrobe in between.

End washroom

If you are looking for an end washroom, bear in mind that the body length in two-berth caravans can be short (usually between 3 and 4m) and closing off the back area will often make things claustrophobic.

In a caravan with separate shower room and wardrobe areas, look for a divider with an inset door. When the divider is in place, it simply closes off the dressing area between the washroom and wardrobe. When you're not using the dressing area, the partition folds back and its door then becomes the entrance to the shower room. This brings the dressing area into the main body of the caravan, making it feel more spacious.

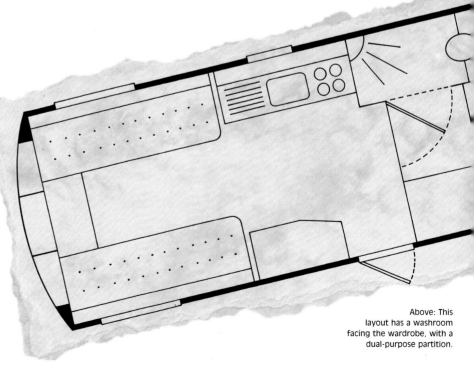

Above: This layout has a washroom facing the wardrobe, with a dual-purpose partition.

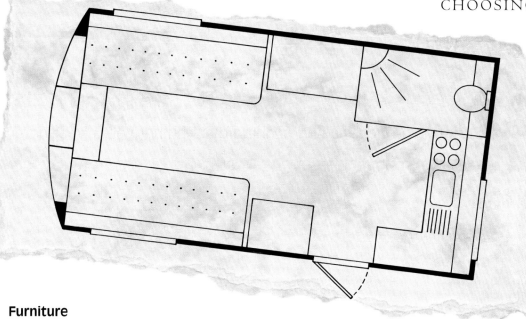

Above: An end kitchen gives plenty of work space.

Furniture

Dresser-style storage units seem to be the preserve of two-berth caravans, which are able to squeeze them in instead of extra sleeping space. Not only do these give extra storage space in the form of shelves, drawers or cupboards, but the top of a unit like this is very useful as a handy TV table or extra work and serving surface.

Because two-berths tend to be bought by older caravanners when their families are grown, and this group generally has more disposable income, a lot of these tourers have luxury features designed to make life much easier. These might include stylish lever taps and huge, slide-out wire baskets for under-bed storage – no need to rummage about under cushions.

End kitchen

Because there are no extra beds or bunks to fit in at the end of the caravan, two-berth caravans often have large kitchens at the back. This can mean a large work surface and plenty of storage space. Usually, an end kitchen takes up most of the width of the caravan, with the washroom in one corner. Because the caravan toilet is in the washroom, this is not an arrangement that suits everyone!

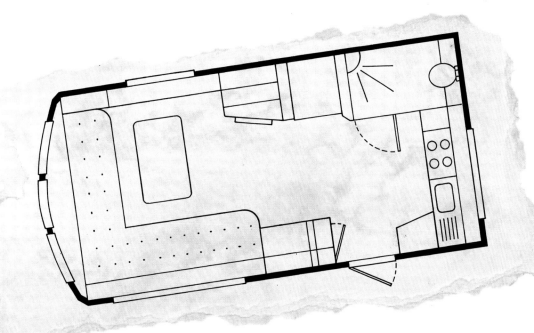

WHICH LAYOUT?

When choosing a layout, be as practical as possible.

- Try to make up the beds and see if there are any **AWKWARD CUSHION SHAPES** or gaps that might make you uncomfortable in the night. What is the headroom like, especially towards the front of the caravan?

- If there is an **END KITCHEN NEXT TO A WASHROOM**, do cupboard, oven or washroom doors bang into each other when opened at the same time? This could lead to accidents

- In layouts where the **KITCHEN IS CENTRAL**, is there room for others to pass while the cook is busy?

- Where are the **WINDOWS POSITIONED**, and are there plenty of roof lights?

- Are there any areas of the caravan **WHERE DAYLIGHT CAN'T GET IN**? If so, is there good artificial lighting?

TWO-BERTH FACTS

- **WEIGHT ALLOWANCES** can be more generous in two-berth caravans. This is because they are generally lighter due to their smaller size

- **ONLY TWO PEOPLE** can sleep in a two-berther. If you want to take more people, add an awning to give you extra sleeping space

- A **SHORTER BODY LENGTH** means less living space

- **EXTRA BEDS** cannot be fitted to two-berthers, so be absolutely sure you'll never need extra berths before you buy

Left: L-shaped seating means that there is ample room for stretching out.

Single or twin axle?

Most caravans have a single axle and just two wheels, but the bigger – and therefore the heavier – the caravan, the more likely it is to have a twin axle and four wheels to spread the weight more evenly on the tyres. If you are buying a large caravan it will probably have a twin axle, although some smaller, lighter caravans are now also built on four wheels.

SINGLE AXLE

Advantages

Most caravans are adequately supported by one axle. Manoeuvrability is the biggest bonus. If you want to swing a single-axle caravan right round on itself you can – it simply pivots on its 'inside' wheel. Because single axles are generally smaller and lighter than twin axles, it is quite possible for two people to push them onto a pitch or into a storage space by hand without too much effort.

Disadvantages

A single axle lends itself to a sort of see-saw motion from nose to tail when the caravan is stationary, so always remember to put down the corner steadies before you step inside if the caravan is unhitched. Otherwise it may 'sit down' with you inside – not a very pleasant experience! Two tyres on each side give better on-road grip than one, so a twin axle should be more stable.

TWIN AXLE

Advantages

Greater resistance to side wind pressure and better on-road grip gives the twin axle more stability while towing. The extra living space afforded by these big caravans makes them suitable for long-term touring if you're planning to stay on site for a considerable length of time. If you suffer a puncture, you still have three tyres, so it may be feasible to drive cautiously to a safe spot to change the wheel.

Disadvantages

As well as the initial cost of a larger caravan and the extra weight, there are twice as many tyres to replace. You will also need a large towcar. Larger caravans cost more in tolls and ferry fares, and in some countries there are maximum length limits. The extra grip of a twin axle is a liability when trying to manoeuvre by hand – turning causes one inside wheel to 'scrub', that is, resist the movement.

Easy-tow tourers

To some people, the size of a caravan can seem daunting. They may perceive problems with towing a large box 2.5m high and 2.1m wide, or with having the room at home to store it. But there are alternatives available, specifically designed to be easy to handle, tow and store while still providing all the benefits of ordinary touring caravans.

PLUS POINTS

- **COMPACT CARAVANS ARE LIGHT**, so they don't need a huge car to tow them

- The **LOW HEIGHT** of folding caravans on the road means that they have a low centre of gravity and therefore greater stability

- Folding and 'pop-top' caravans are low enough to **FIT INTO A GARAGE**. Some folding caravans can even be tipped on their side and 'hung' from a garage wall

- Because **LITTLE WIND RESISTANCE** is offered by folding tourers and pop-tops, fuel economy is far better than with a rigid-sided tourer

- It will take one person just a **FEW MINUTES** to erect a folding caravan

MOTOR CARAVANS

You can do away with towing totally if you choose a motor caravan, which can be converted from a panel van or similar car, or comes ready-built onto a vehicle chassis. The main disadvantage with motor caravans is that you don't have the flexibility of separate transport – if you want to sight-see or simply visit the shops, then you have to pack everything up each time. The height and length of these vehicles can also be a problem for town parking.

PUTTING UP A FOLDING CARAVAN

Starting to unfold

1 Once you are on site and have unhitched the folding caravan from the car and applied the caravan handbrake, you can start to erect the unit. It's wise to put the corner steadies down, too. Now undo the catches that hold the roof down.

One end at a time

2 Lift up one of the ends of the caravan (which should glide up easily on its gas struts – just like those you get on car hatches) and lock into place once it is fully extended. Repeat for the other end.

Putting up the sides

3 It is usually better to start with the side that contains the door, so that you can step into the caravan and stand inside the door frame. Pulling the side up towards you and then pushing it into place minimizes the effort needed.

'Pop-top'

Similar to a conventional caravan, pop-tops have a roof section that you raise once on site to give more headroom along almost the entire length of the caravan. They have the advantage of being much lower than traditional tourers when on the road, although not quite as low as a folding caravan, and are often very light – this model weighs just 590kg. Taller caravanners should note that the doorways are often lower than those on traditional tourers.

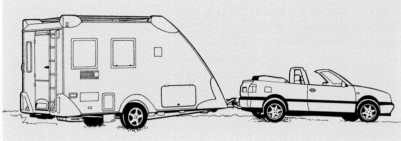

Compact caravan

If you'd like a traditional tourer but also want something that's easy to tow and small enough to be manoeuvred single-handed on site, look out for these mini versions. Average lengths are 4m from hitchhead to end. These compact caravans are well-equipped and ideal for those with active outdoor lifestyles – the German model shown here is designed to carry cycles or a motorbike inside.

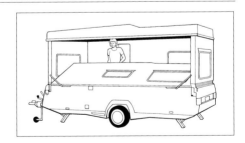

The final touches

4 Erect the last side by standing inside the caravan, pulling it up into place, and then locking it into position. Finally, lift the roof lockers and units into their correct positions and hang any curtain pelmets.

Folding caravan

This is basically a rigid tourer with sides that can be folded down to give it the towing dimensions of a car trailer. The roof forms a 'lid' that closes over the body for towing. All the usual facilities are included, such as a hob, fridge, 12V lighting and mains electrics. The cupboards and the kitchen unit have to be below the 'folding' line while the caravan is being towed and are raised into position once you are on site.

Buying new

If you're lucky enough to be able to buy a new caravan, then you will be presented with a huge choice of different options – so huge that making the correct final decision can sometimes be problematic. The following pointers should take some of the stress out of buying new.

Caravan warranties

When buying a new caravan, try to get the longest warranty you can. Then, if a major fault develops early in the caravan's life, you will be covered. Look for at least three years and if the manufacturer is offering a five-year warranty, all the better. When considering a particular make of caravan, study the warranty conditions carefully. Most manufacturers make annual servicing – at a service centre that has their approval – a condition of the warranty. If this work is not carried out according to the terms of the warranty and a fault does develop, manufacturers are within their rights to dishonour a claim for repair under that warranty.

Above: It is often well worth taking children with you when you choose your tourer – they are at just the right height to notice things such as sharp corners on furniture.

A wide choice

When you are choosing a used caravan your main priority is getting the newest model in the best condition that you can afford. With a new caravan it is basically a question of finding something to your taste within your budget. The choice, however, can be overwhelming. Visit a few local dealerships that stock a wide range of franchises and bring home all the brochures you can. Look at the differences in equipment levels and what you get for your money in comparable ranges from different manufacturers.

Decision-making

You may be the one who is actually financing the purchase of the caravan, but it isn't just you who will be using it – so take along everyone who will be caravanning with you when you go to choose your tourer. Children have a unique perspective and often spot things – sharp edges, impractical catches, surfaces that they cannot reach and so on – that make the caravan unsuitable for family use. Also, if anyone who will be touring with you takes an instant dislike to the model you propose to buy, imagine how they will feel after spending their summer holidays in it.

Testing it out

Taking a caravan out for a test drive, as you would with a car, seldom happens. Dealers don't usually have the insurance cover or the facilities to allow you to do this. If you are a newcomer to caravanning, the chances are that you won't have had a towbar fitted to your car yet; if you do have one, a quick tow around the block won't tell you what it will be like to live in a particular tourer over two weeks touring round the country. The best preparation you can do is to work out your outfit-matching sums carefully (see pages 56-59) and take plenty of time to inspect each area of the caravan for comfort and practicality.

- **CHOOSE YOUR SOURCE OF FINANCE WITH CARE**. Do you have cash? Paying outright is the best way to buy, although few buyers can afford this

  The dealer may offer credit – look at the small print and the charge for credit carefully. Is it really a good option?

  What rates does your bank or building society lend at? Some have very competitive terms

  If you are taking out a loan or credit agreement, how long will it run for? Bear in mind that, to get the best deal on another new caravan by trading-in, you should look to change your tourer within five years

- Look out for **SPECIAL EDITIONS**. They are usually around the same price as the standard models, but carry a different model name and give you more comfort and equipment for your money. These extras could be highly valuable at trade-in time

- **BE CAREFUL AT AUCTIONS** – as with car auctions, take someone with you who really knows the field. Auctions are notorious for being places where dealers offload unwanted or cannibalized stock

- Remember, the caravan that you finally choose should be your **KEY TO FREEDOM**, and not any kind of millstone round your neck

Left, above and below: Don't be afraid to have a really thorough look around everything in the caravan, and put its comfort to the test if at all possible. After all, this will be your home for reasonable stretches of time. Try the beds for length, and get any bunks out to see what they are like for weight and size.

Buying used

Not everyone can afford to buy a brand-new caravan. There's no reason at all why buying used shouldn't provide you with a tourer that is in top condition, able to give you years of touring pleasure. All you have to do is know what you're looking for and use common sense to find the caravan that fits both your needs and your budget.

WHAT TO LOOK FOR

Watch out for signs of damp

1 Damp problems usually occur when a seal on the caravan's exterior fails and lets water in. If left untreated, damp will rot away any wood in the structure and cause fatal damage. A tell-tale, sickly sweet smell is usually a late sign – damp is known as 'caravan cancer' as external signs are hard to spot. Look in the back corners of roof lockers and under beds – both front and back – for discoloration of the wall covering or wood.

Check over the chassis

2 Dirt suggests a careless owner, while steadies that don't descend smoothly might mean that they have been used to level the tourer – or that an accident has bent the chassis. Look for corrosion on steel chassis; aluminium ones won't rust, but may be pitted by road salt. Galvanized chassis are almost maintenance-free; a good clean removes any 'rust'.

Is it stolen?

3 Locate the number on the metal plate bolted onto the caravan near the door, or die-stamped on the chassis. This will tell you the caravan's age (check with the manufacturer that this information corresponds with what the vendor says). If this number has been tampered with, the caravan may have been stolen.

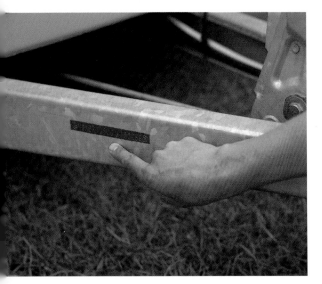

Inspect the towing hitch

4 Does the handle on top of the hitchhead lift easily and is the breakaway cable and other cabling intact? Does the handbrake hold the caravan when fully engaged? Are the electrical pins free from damage and corrosion deposits (this could cause a bad connection between car and caravan). Pull on the D-shaped handles used for hand manoeuvring. If they aren't firm, this may be a sign of damp.

Look out for body damage

5 Has the caravan had an accident? Unlike a car, the dents in a caravan cannot be hammered out. A bump against a gatepost can mean a whole new side, and this is extremely expensive. Any scratches that have punctured the skin may let water in and lead to damp if untreated. Is the mastic in its seams dry and crumbly? If so, it will need replacing.

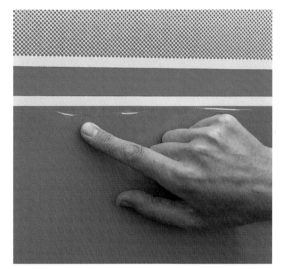

How good are the tyres?

6 Look for even wear and good tread depth across the tyre. Perished or cracked tyres are the sign of a negligent owner. Remember to check the inside of the tyre, too. Question any deep scuff marks — if the caravan has been run up against the kerb at speed, then the chassis may be damaged. Is there a spare tyre and a jack (of the correct type) with the caravan? If not, you will need to buy these.

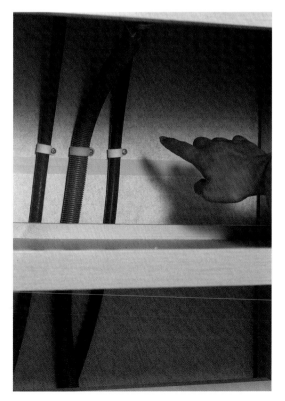

Check that all the systems work

7 Check the plumbing by looking under the kitchen unit and at the back of the beds. Can you see any discoloration where water may have leaked? Is the fridge clean and free from mould? Are the burners on the hob rusty? Is there any sign of water leaks or mould in the washroom? If you are buying from a dealer, the gas and electric systems will have been checked and tested. If you aren't buying from a dealer, take the tourer you purchase to an approved service centre as soon as you've bought it, to get the systems checked out and any faults safely rectified before using it at all.

⚠️ HOW CAN I GET THE BEST DEAL?

- If you **ARE A TOTAL NOVICE** where caravans are concerned, take along a knowledgeable adviser. Try to arrange for an inspection by an expert
- **LOOK AT AS MANY** vans of the type you want as possible
- Buy from a **REPUTABLE DEALER** if you can, so that you get a warranty and back-up service
- Does the **CHASSIS PLATE** appear to have been tampered with? If so, check the number with a specialist organization or your local police
- With a private sale, make sure you get some protection by asking for **A RECEIPT** that describes the van's condition
- Check with a specialist firm that there is **NO OUTSTANDING FINANCE** on the caravan

THE INTERIOR

Soft furnishings should be clean and firm, although re-upholstering is always an option. Check that taps and knobs don't come off in your hand. Lift any rugs – they may cover bald patches or stains on the carpet. Watch out for cracks in windows – replacement can be both tricky and costly.

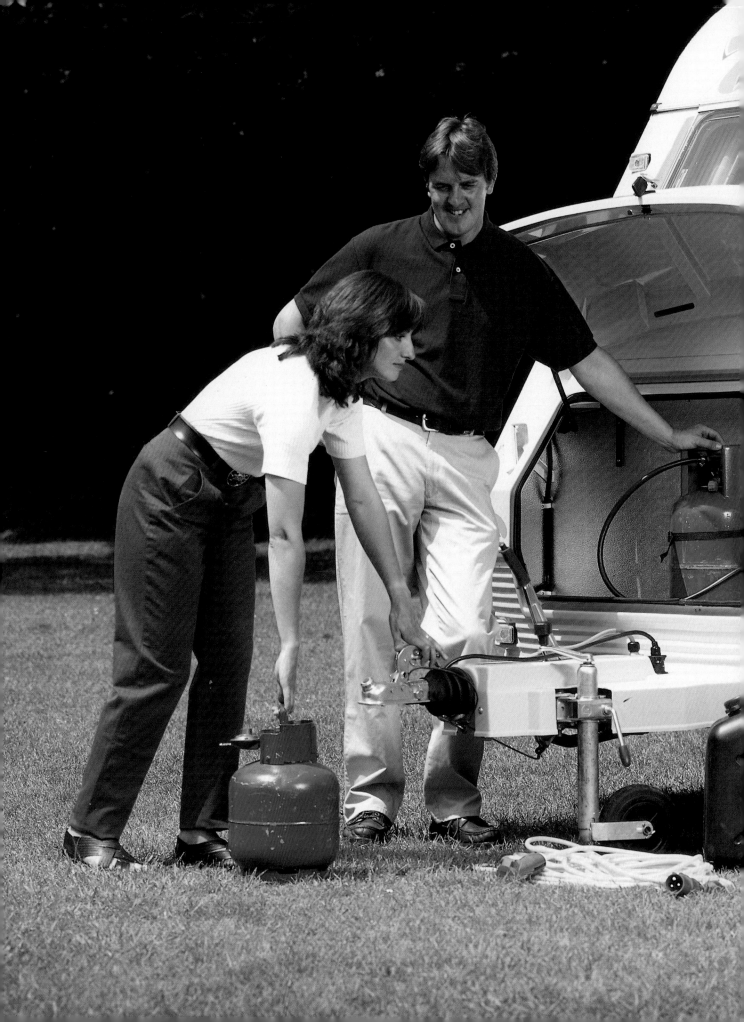

CHAPTER 3

Caravan ACCESSORIES

Some gadgets are essential purchases. Without them, you wouldn't be able to use and live in your caravan – you might even be breaking the law. Others, like awnings, which can double the amount of available living space in your caravan, are designed to make life on site a little easier. Products that improve your caravan's safety and security will give you peace of mind. Make sure you buy the essentials and then take time to consider the merits of the rest.

Your accessories should prepare you for everyday occurrences such as bad weather as well as more serious hazards

The essential kit

So, you now have your caravan – but wait a minute before you try to take to the open road. You won't be able to use your holiday home at all without buying certain essential accessories and there are all kinds of additional items that will improve both safety and security.

Setting up on site

You certainly can't caravan without a winder for letting down the steadies (legs) at each corner of the caravan – or your caravan will rock violently when you climb inside! A specially designed set of steps makes getting in and out easy. If one of the wheels is in a slight dip, a pair of ramps will help you level the caravan. Don't forget a torch if you're arriving on site at night.

Waste water container

This is where all the water goes when you've had a shower or run a tap. The dirty water flows through the caravan's waste pipes to an outlet (usually at the back of the caravan) and then into the container via a length of black connecting pipe. There are two openings on the container, both with screw-top lids. Use the side opening as an inlet (water drains easily into here when the container is placed on its side) and the top one for emptying.

Your power supply

Caravans have three possible power sources – mains electricity, electricity from a battery and gas from an on-board supply. The cable shown here connects to the caravan at one end and the site's mains supply at the other. The battery is a special one for use with caravans and is carried inside it. Caravan gas is readily available at most caravan sites and at petrol stations, where an empty cylinder is exchanged for a full one.

Number plate and towing mirrors

Your caravan must carry a number plate – bearing the same registration mark as your car – and it must be lit like your car's. Towing – or 'extension' – mirrors are essential on most cars to give a clear view to the back of the caravan and of traffic behind. A car's mirrors won't let you see past the width of most caravans. Simply fix extension mirrors onto the existing mirrors or the wing of your car whenever you're towing.

Fresh water container and water pump

This container holds your drinking water supply. Water is heavy and carrying a full container across a caravan site is hard work. This version comes with a handle and a pipe for filling it from the site tap. Once it's full, flip it onto its side, attach the handle, and pull it back to the caravan. If you buy a square container, there are special trolleys that you can strap it to for transportation, but they can be bulky and heavy. Don't forget a submersible pump, to get the water from the container into the caravan.

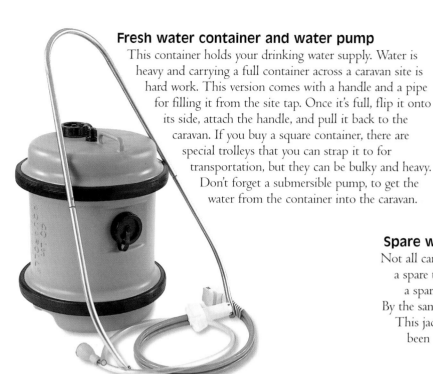

Spare wheel and jack

Not all caravans come with a spare tyre as standard, so make sure you buy one, and a spare wheel for it to go on. A car spare won't do the job. By the same token, most car jacks are not suitable for caravans. This jack is made by a caravan chassis manufacturer and has been designed for use with a caravan. Your manufacturer's handbook will show you jacking points, if your caravan has them.

Security devices

The message here is 'the more the merrier', and you should fit them every time you leave your caravan – even on site or while you're having a break at a motorway service station. Fitting more than one device will make theft harder and can act as a visual deterrent to a would-be thief. A sturdy wheelclamp is a sound investment, while a hitchlock does just what it says – locks the hitchhead at the front of the caravan so that no one else can couple up to it and tow it away. (See *Basic Security* pages 46-47.)

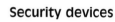

Chemical toilet

If your caravan isn't already fitted with a toilet, or there's not enough room in the washroom to add one, you will probably want one of these portable models, so that you don't have to walk across to the site toilets. Both this portable toilet and the fitted version need additives to function. The chemical for dissolving the waste in the holding tank is usually green or blue. The pink fluid is mixed with water for a flushing action in some models.

> ⚠️ **WHERE DO I BUY THESE?**
>
> - Your local caravan dealer's **ACCESSORY SHOP**
> - New caravans come with a **'WELCOME PACK'** that includes some equipment
> - **MAIL ORDER** or **CLASSIFIED ADVERTS** in local papers and caravan magazines

Bedding and clothing

Unlike certain other pastimes, caravanning means that you can simply take the clothing and bedding that you normally use at home on trips – there's no need to buy anything specially designed for the job. However, there are one or two outdoor hobby items that can come in very useful on a caravanning holiday and may be well worth investing in.

BEDDING POINTS

- Always take your bedding **OUT OF THE CARAVAN** after each trip – it may get damp if it is left packed away in lockers

- **SYNTHETIC-FILLED** pillows and duvets are lighter than feather-filled ones, and so save on weight

- Choose **EASILY WASHABLE**, quick-drying bedding – you may have to wash it while you're on holiday

- Take more than enough **TOWELS**. You'll need plenty for the beach and for drying off if it rains

- If your **WASHROOM IS HEATED**, open the roof-vent and hang any wet items from the shower rail – they dry very rapidly in the confined space

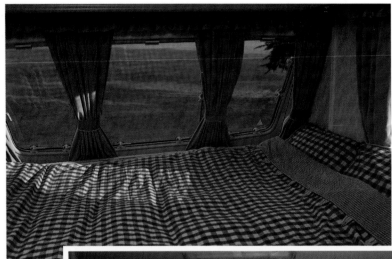

Double beds

Bringing the pillows, sheets and duvet from home is ideal for a double caravan bed. Flat sheets are better than fitted ones, as caravan double beds are often wider than their domestic counterparts. If in doubt, buy king size.

Children's bedding

For a child's single bed or bunk, a pillow and single duvet from home are usually perfectly adequate. If you want to add some 'camping out' excitement, let children take a sleeping bag instead of ordinary bedding. The sleeping bag shown here has an integral pillow and rolls up like a cowboy's bed roll.

Weatherproof wear

A windproof/showerproof coat is essential in case the weather takes a turn for the worst or for caravanning outside the summer months. Choose a fairly lightweight, but warm jacket like the ones seen here.

Keeping warm

Fleece tops, worn here under the waterproof jackets, are perfect for caravanners as they can be built up in layers and peeled off again when the wearer gets warm. Fleeces come in different weights, from lightweight (for using as layers and when staying close to the caravan) up to heavyweight (for serious walking at low temperatures).

Wellington boots

Wellingtons are essential. Even sites that offer hard pitching surfaces instead of the usual field will probably have large grassy areas. One rainstorm and you could be in a quagmire. Stand your boots upside down on sticks, ready to be washed clean by the next shower, while staying dry inside.

Fire safety

In the compact space of a caravan, it's important that you take all the fire safety precautions possible. Because a caravan is constructed from very combustible materials such as wood, fire can spread rapidly. A caravan also carries its own gas and has equipment that works off a supply of electricity, and these types of fire require careful treatment.

FIRE-FIGHTING

- **CHOOSE AN EXTINGUISHER** with a gauge that shows you if it has lost pressure

- **DON'T SCRIMP** – it's worth buying quality to ensure safety

- **MAKE SURE EVERYONE** who uses the caravan knows where the extinguisher is and how to operate it

- **IF THERE IS A FIRE INVOLVING GAS**, just get everyone out of the caravan, and don't try to fight it. Only turn off the gas if there is no risk to you

- **NEVER USE** an extinguisher on a fat fire – use a fire blanket

- **ALWAYS CHECK YOUR FIRE EXTINGUISHERS** before you set out

- **CHECK THE DATE** on your extinguisher, to make sure that it is not too old

- **DON'T MOUNT** an extinguisher near a likely source of flames – you might not be able to get to it if a fire breaks out

Fire extinguisher

Because fire extinguishers are designed for fighting different types of fire, it's important that you choose the right one for tackling the sort of fires you are likely to get in a caravan. These are usually Class A (wood, textiles, fabrics and paper) and Class C (flammable gases). Most caravan fires also involve electricity, so the best type to deal with all of these scenarios is a dry powder extinguisher. A 600g to 1kg extinguisher is big enough – the idea is to use the extinguisher to keep the fire at bay while you and your family get out of the caravan, not necessarily to put it out.

Smoke alarm

If you haven't got a smoke alarm in your caravan, fit one. Just like at home, you and your family could be sound asleep when a fire starts. Because you can get smoke alarms with a sticky pad on the back for fixing to surfaces without any drilling or screws, you can easily put one in the most appropriate place. An alarm tends to be ultra-sensitive in a caravan because it will be much closer to sources of smoke than at home. Don't be tempted to take the battery out – you could forget to replace it – and carry a spare.

Right: The best place to position a fire extinguisher is between the kitchen – where the fire is likely to start – and the external door. If you are fitting a smoke alarm, put it as close to the kitchen as you can without it being so close that smoke from ordinary cooking sets it off.

Fire blanket

For kitchen fires where an extinguisher isn't appropriate, such as fat fires, use a fire blanket. Very few caravan manufacturers fit them as standard but they are relatively inexpensive and can be fixed easily to the kitchen wall. Make sure that you won't have to reach over the hob to get to the fire blanket – this could be dangerous if there is a pan fire. Pull the tabs to release the blanket and, holding it so that it is rolled protectively around your hands, use it to smother the fire.

WHAT SHOULD I DO?

- **IF THE GAS GOES OUT** while you're cooking, always turn off the appliance and wait before re-lighting

- **DON'T TACKLE A FIRE** unless you have to. Get everyone out quickly

- **IMMERSE BURNS** in cold water, under a running tap

- If you think you have **A GAS LEAK**, turn off the supply, then take caravan to a service centre

Towing mirrors

As caravans are generally wider than their towcars, it can be very difficult to see traffic coming from behind. The rules vary around the world, from countries where it is a legal requirement to fit at least one additional extension mirror to your car, to those that simply recommend that you do so. Whatever the case, it is always much safer to use them – a pair if possible.

THROUGH VISION

Some caravans with large rear windows allow the towcar driver to see right through the caravan via the car's rear-view mirror. This means that the tops of cars, and a good portion of larger vehicles such as lorries, are visible. The big advantage of having through vision is that you are more aware of all-round traffic conditions – you see what's behind you before it suddenly tries to overtake.

Basic clip-on

This style of mirror is the cheapest and the easiest to fit, and can be attached to most ordinary car mirrors. It features two arms with small hooks that clip over the surround of the car mirror. Two

notched rubber straps run across the back of the car mirror, from the top arm of the towing mirror to its bottom arm. On each strap is a tightening device, so you can tighten the straps notch by notch until the mirror is firmly in place – otherwise, vibration while towing could easily loosen it.

Door attachment

A mirror designed to fit directly onto the car door. A hook at the top of the bracket slides into the small space between the car door and window and a rubber strap is pulled down to hook

under the bottom of the door. Strap length can be adjusted to fit the door's depth, keeping the mirror firmly in place, with little movement when you are towing. One disadvantage of this mirror is that it is bulky, and dust behind the central arm can scratch paintwork.

Car wing attachment

To attach this mirror to your car, you have to open the bonnet so that you can secure two clips over the top of the car's wing. Another clip at the bottom of the assembly hooks under the

wheel arch and the mirror is then bolted to the arm part of the assembly. The main 'pro' of this mirror is that just a slight movement of the eyes is needed to look in it; the 'cons' are that you cannot adjust the mirror angle from the driver's seat, and it is quite bulky to store.

Swivel-arm

This is the ideal design for cars with larger mirrors or for owners of off-roaders who still want to fit a towing mirror. In this model, a strap runs across the back of the car mirror. It is fixed to a tube

that clips onto the top of the car mirror, clipped over the bottom of the mirror, and then tightened. The towing mirror itself swivels on a long arm that fits into the tube and is secured with a nut. There is little movement and the adjustable arm means you can position the mirror where you like.

Basic security

Caravan theft, like car theft, is on the increase. Unfortunately, as a relatively lightweight leisure vehicle, a caravan doesn't come with a range of security features as standard, and this can make it an easy target. However, there are all kinds of highly effective devices that you can fit yourself. Decide which ones are best for your needs before you buy.

WHAT CAN I DO?

- **DETER THIEVES** by fitting a range of security devices

- **FIT GATES** at the bottom of your drive if you usually store your caravan here

- **PARK YOUR CAR** across the end of the drive to deter thieves further

- Fit an **OUTDOOR SECURITY LIGHT** to help prevent night-time theft

- **INSURE YOUR CARAVAN** as soon as you buy it

- **REMEMBER THAT YOU'RE NEVER SAFE** from thieves – even during a brief break at a motorway service area

- **ETCH THE CARAVAN WINDOWS** with its chassis number, if it hasn't already been etched in

- **KEEP A NOTE** of the chassis number at home

- **BUY A PEN** that shows up only in ultraviolet light and mark inside lockers and under furniture

- **KEEP A LIST** of any distinguishing features – accessories and equipment you may have added, any bumps and scratches on the bodywork and so on. Pass these on to the police if the caravan is stolen

- **TAKE OFF THE WHEELS** if you won't be using the caravan for a while

- **ON A HOME SECURITY NOTE:** Get neighbours to look out for you while you're away on your caravanning holiday – if you keep a caravan outside your house and it suddenly disappears for two weeks, it can be an open advertisement to a burglar

HITCHLOCKS

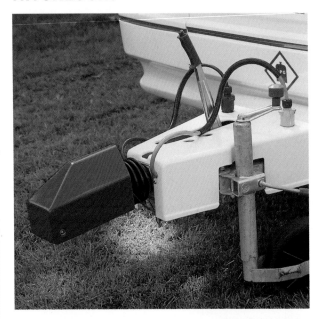

Standard hitchlock

A hitchlock locks the hitchhead, or 'coupling head', so that thieves cannot simply hitch up your caravan to their own car and drive it away. Basically, all hitchlocks try to stop a thief from:

a) lifting the handle on the hitchhead in order to hitch up

b) being able to put the towball of their own towcar under the hitchhead so that they can then hitch up and drive away. Some hitchlocks, like this one, cover up as much of the hitchhead as possible – it has been known for thieves to undo the bolts holding the head in place, discard it (with the lock still on it) and then fix a new hitchhead on in its place so that they can hitch up and go.

Dual-purpose hitchlock

This hitchlock has a dual purpose – as well as using it when your caravan is unhitched, it can be used while the caravan and car are coupled up. (It mustn't, however, be used while you are moving; restricting the coupling like this and not allowing the caravan to break free if it has to is unsafe practice.) This type of lock is especially useful if you have to stop for a break while on the road. Simply place the lock over the coupling, slide the pin into position and lock it. Then, when the caravan is unhitched, on site or at home, turn the lock until it is horizontal and fit it over the hitchhead.

WHEELCLAMPS

Heavy-duty wheelclamp

Always look for a wheelclamp that is well-made and substantial. This heavy-duty model is very solid, which means that it's also fairly expensive. Its solidity makes it quite heavy, so it is probably best suited to a caravan that is stored for long periods of time between holidays. The central plate fits over the wheel nuts. This means that a thief cannot undo the nuts and remove the wheel in an attempt to get rid of the clamp.

Multi-purpose wheelclamp

Quite modestly priced, this clamp will probably find many uses around the home. It has been designed to clamp everything from a motorbike wheel to a car, caravan or panel van wheel. It has two strengthened steel arms that reach around tyres up to 23cm in width and then slot together for locking into place. Lightweight in comparison to many other clamps, this style is ideal for taking away caravanning, where you need to watch your weight. Because it is so quick and easy to fit, it can also be taken out and used en route — when the outfit is parked at a rest area, for example.

Easy-adjust wheelclamp

Again, this lock covers the wheel nuts and cradles the wheel securely. Its solid looks are a good visual deterrent. This type of clamp may seem expensive initially, but if your caravan is going to be left unattended for fairly long periods of time, such as in storage over winter, then it may prove well worth the money. Another advantage of this type of clamp is that it is highly adjustable and so easy to fit.

Other security devices

As well as obvious safeguards such as hitchlocks and wheelclamps, there are many other effective security devices on the market. Extra locks and alarms to detect intruders or any movements of the caravan can help prevent theft in the first place, while electronic tagging might enable you to recover your caravan if the worst happens.

SAFE STORAGE

If you are unlikely to use your caravan for long periods, it's best to store it where it is protected against thieves (and the elements). Storage sites range from a farm barn with a lock on the door to those that are purpose-built and highly secure.

Mid-way between these are caravan sites that also have an area set aside for storage. Caravanners sometimes buy a pitch for the season, storing their caravan on the site so that, whenever they want to use it, the park owner fetches it out for them and stows it away again afterwards.

HOW SECURE?

Check out the security arrangements carefully – does anyone live on the premises or is it patrolled regularly? Remember that pass key systems can often be overcome by thieves. Security fencing, floodlights, guard dogs, alarm systems and security barriers all help to keep thieves out. The most secure storage sites are not those that advertise, but ones passed on by word of mouth.

Corner steady lock

This small lock doesn't involve any drilling or fixing – just a couple of minutes' time to slot it into place and lock it. What it does is lock the steady in the down position so that it can't be wound up by a potential thief in order to tow the caravan away. Trying to tow away a caravan with this device fitted correctly is almost impossible without damaging the chassis. Some caravan manufacturers fit these locks as standard to one of the caravan's back legs.

Infra-red alarm

This alarm system consists of a control panel (the keypad); a PIR (Passive Infra-Red) unit that detects the body heat of an intruder; a powerful 118-decibel siren; and two 'reed' door contacts that fit either side of openings (such as the caravan door or gas locker) and trigger the alarm when the door is opened.

The keypad is the heart of the system, operating on a code of your choice from 1 to 12 digits. Once set up, the alarm gives you 15 seconds to leave the caravan and, on return, 15 seconds to key in the code and prevent the alarm going off.

It has been designed so that potential thieves keying in random numbers to defeat the alarm will be detected by an 'invalid code sensor'. This will set off the alarm if the wrong code is entered more than twice.

By wiring the system into the car's towing sockets the alarm will go off when the car's doors or tailgate are opened, or if the caravan plugs are taken out of the car's sockets. The system operates on two batteries, which are fitted in the siren unit.

Movement alarms

This alarm runs off the caravan's battery and has a number of standard features to detect movement inside the caravan as well as movement of the caravan itself. Once the alarm is triggered, the siren will sound – at 110 decibels. A sensor is fitted to one of the rear corner steadies so that winding it up triggers the alarm. Inserting the electrical connection(s) into a towcar will also set it off, as will the first use of the footbrake after setting off. The alarm comes with a pressure mat that goes under the carpet (usually just inside the door) and triggers the alarm when trodden on.

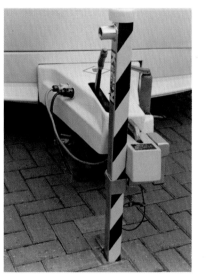
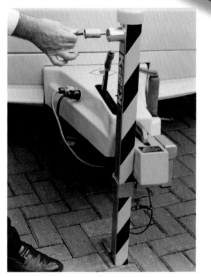

Security posts

If you keep your caravan in your driveway when it's not in use, a security post could help prevent it from being stolen. A solid steel post usually locks into a 'socket' that is concreted-in underground. These posts may have a T-bar at the top to stop the caravan being moved or, more usually, a facility that enables you to hitchlock the caravan and then secure the hitchlock itself to the post.

Letter codes

Marking a code in large letters on the roof of your tourer can help in tracking it down if it's stolen – the code can be seen from bridges and police helicopters. Some companies supply letters and numbers in reflective or fluorescent material, so that the codes work both day and night. Police forces advise that you don't use your postcode. This is because it's easy for thieves to source postcodes and to know that a caravanner's house is lying empty while they are away on holiday.

Electronic tagging

What happens if, despite your precautions, your caravan is still stolen? An electronic tagging system, using a small microchip placed inside the caravan, is one method that is proving highly successful. In general terms, a computer database of registered owners allows the scanning and checking of a suspicious caravan. One tagging system is activated by the owner contacting a central database. Police vehicles fitted with direction finders can then hunt for the caravan.

Right: The microchip used in electronic tagging systems, shown here at its actual size.

Home comforts

Caravans offer two sources of power for appliances – mains electricity from a site hook-up or 12V from the battery, or both. Many of the appliances you use at home are suitable for your caravan, or there are special, low-electricity consumption variants that are ideal for caravan use. Work out how much power they will need before you plug in!

Travel iron

If you have to iron while you're on holiday – perhaps for a special night out – then you will find that a small travel iron is very light, takes up little space and uses low wattage. The handle on the iron shown here folds down, so it can be packed flat, and it also has a steam facility.

Additional heater

Very useful when winter caravanning to conserve your gas supply and keep the chill off the caravan. Choose carefully – the type of convector heater shown here doesn't have any exposed elements, which pose a fire risk in a caravan. It draws very few watts and can be used at the same time as most low-wattage TVs and kettles.

Stereo radio-cassette

The majority of touring caravans don't have a stereo fitted. Where they do it's usually a car radio-cassette player and speakers, as there is no such thing as a 'caravan stereo'. So a portable radio-cassette is really useful, especially as it can be run on mains or batteries – handy if your site has no electrics.

Hair-dryer

A hair-dryer draws a very high wattage, even in a small travel version. This one uses 1200W – domestic hair-dryers can draw around 3000 – but still has two powerful settings. The handle collapses for easy packing.

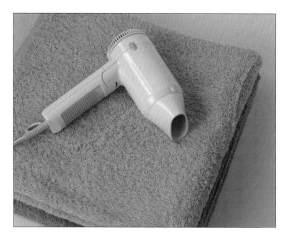

HOW MUCH POWER?

- Work out how much of **YOUR AMP 'ALLOCATION'** you will use: Amps = watts divided by volts. For example, a 600W appliance, running off mains (for example, 230V), uses 2.6 amps

- **A GENERATOR** like the one on the right is an alternative to a mains hook-up. They are sold in wattage outputs, and those giving between 300 and 900W are generally best for caravanners

- Take a note of **THE WATTS NEEDED** to power the appliances you run simultaneously. This will give you the minimum rated output in watts that you require of a generator – start-up current in some appliances may be greater than running current

Computer

If you can't leave all your work behind when you head off for a break, then take the lap-top with you. Most models work perfectly well off mains electrics but, again, watch what other appliances you use at the same time. Like the radio-cassette, it has the added bonus that it can be used on battery power if the need arises.

Kettle

A domestic kettle isn't suitable for caravan use – it has an element of at least 2000W. But a kettle specially designed for low consumption – like this travel version – is fine. If you want to remove the kettle from the electricity equation altogether, try using the kind that you put on a gas burner.

Portable television

A portable TV from home may be fine for your caravan – check its consumption. Or you could buy a TV like this one, which runs off 12V. Some combination TV-videos are also suitable for caravans. (See pages 160-161.)

An extra room

If you're buying a small caravan but would like the option of taking extra people with you from time to time, you'll need the caravan version of guest bedrooms – the awning. Made from either cotton or acrylic (sometimes both), it can be used any way you like, for enlarging your dining area perhaps, or for storing large items such as bicycles.

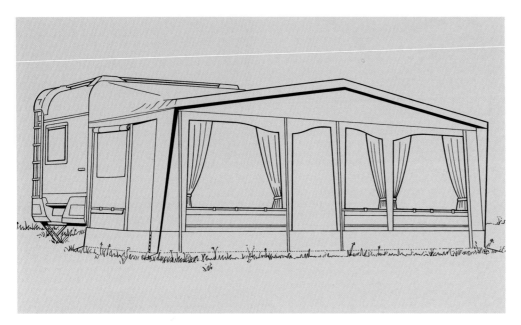

Full awning

A full awning goes right from one end of the caravan to the other and effectively doubles your available living space. The front and sides may have panels that can be removed in summer to turn the awning into a cool sun shade, or zipped in during the cooler months to keep out wind and rain. Inner 'bedroom' compartments can be bought for this type of awning, but many caravanners use it as an al fresco dining area. A full awning does take a while to erect and take down, so it is best suited to those spending their whole holiday more or less on one site.

Porch awning

If you'd like an awning but will be touring around, then a porch awning could be the right choice. Fitting over the door area and acting just like the porch at home, it's also useful for storing muddy boots and wet jackets. Some caravanners have a full awning for their main holiday and take a porch awning on shorter trips.

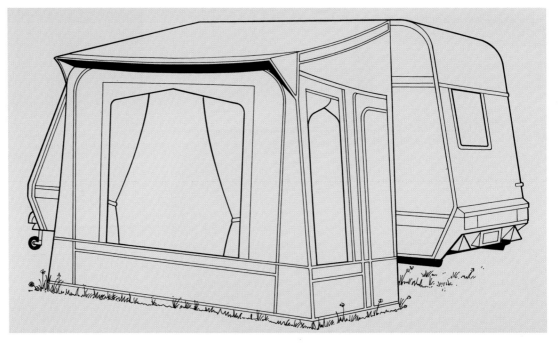

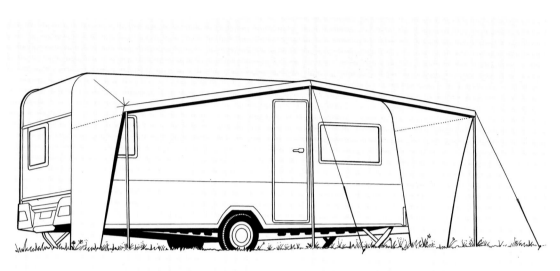

Sunshade

If you plan to do a lot of touring in warm countries, this is the perfect option. It's small, lightweight and can be erected in minutes. Throwing a shadow over one side of the caravan, it creates a cool retreat from the heat, which is ideal for families with young children. It will also provide some protection from summer rainstorms, sheltering food and dinner guests!

MEASURING UP

When buying an awning, make sure that you know the make, model and year of your tourer. The manufacturer of either your caravan or the awning should then be able to give you the right size. A few centimetres too small and your awning won't fit; a few centimetres too big and it will sag and collect rain.

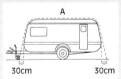

HOW TO CHECK THE SIZE
You can check that the size is correct by finding out your 'A' measurement, as follows. Site the caravan on level ground. Now measure from ground level at the most forward point of the awning channel, right around the channel to its most rearward point, and then down to the ground. (This channel runs along the top and sides of the door side of a tourer.) The start and finish points should be 30cm in front of and 30cm behind where the channel would reach if it extended down to the ground.

Winter awning

Usually made from heavy polyester and PVC, these awnings are designed specifically to be used during the winter months. Ordinary awnings are not suitable for this — anyone sleeping in one while it is snowing would probably have an extremely chilly night. A heavyweight option is particularly useful for people who enjoy winter sports. The integral roof helps snow slide off, extra support poles are available to improve strength (in case of extreme weather and heavy snowfalls) and it is big enough for storing skis and poles.

CHAPTER 4

Weight
WATCHING

The weight of your caravan is extremely important. Don't be tempted to buy the biggest, best-equipped caravan you can find – you will probably discover that your car won't be able to pull it more than a couple of metres. What you should look for is a caravan with enough loading allowance to enable you to take what you need with you – remember that a badly- or over-loaded caravan is a danger on the road. A few sums before you buy will help you keep your weight down.

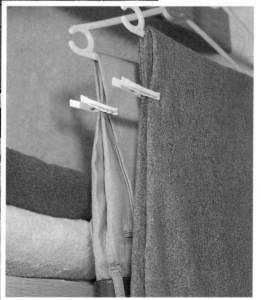

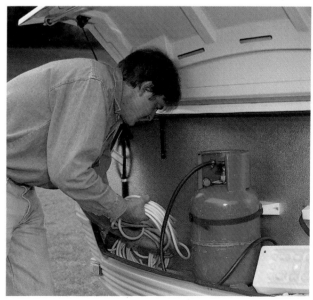

Find out how heavy your tourer and its contents should be, and which packing strategies will work best

Car and caravan matching

One of the basics of caravanning is getting your weight ratios correct. The weight and engine size of your car dictate the size of caravan that it can tow, and if you buy a caravan that is too heavy it may damage your car or make you a danger on the road. Find out your car's capabilities and then choose the right car-caravan pairing.

The right balance

This caravan, fully laden, weighs less than the car's kerbweight (see *What Weights?*, opposite). This means that the car will suffer minimal strain and will always be in control if you ever run into any difficulties. A properly matched car-and-caravan 'outfit' handles well on the road and makes touring simple and stress-free. Doing a few quick sums correctly will enable you to drive up and down hills with ease, cruise along motorways and cope with winding country lanes.

The wrong balance

This is a recipe for disaster. The fully laden caravan is far heavier than the car, so if the outfit gets into any difficulties on the road, the caravan will dictate the whole outfit's movement. For example, caught in a strong crosswind on an open stretch of road, the caravan may start to sway. A heavier car that is properly matched to the caravan would cope easily and dampen down the movement. A badly matched car, such as this one, will follow the caravan's movement, making a crash much more likely.

THE 85% RECOMMENDATION

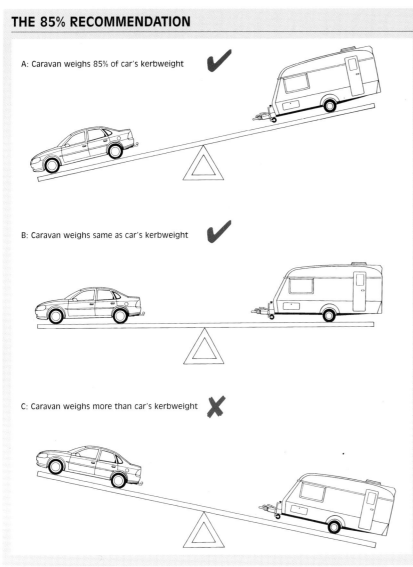

A: Caravan weighs 85% of car's kerbweight

B: Caravan weighs same as car's kerbweight ✔

C: Caravan weighs more than car's kerbweight ✘

- It is usually recommended that a caravan, fully laden, should weigh **BETWEEN 85% AND 100%** of the car's kerbweight (see box, right)

- As a general guide, conventional petrol engines with a capacity **UP TO 1500CC** should be adequate for towing a fully laden caravan weighing 85% of the car's kerbweight (see illustration A)

- **ABOVE 1500CC**, engines should manage a caravan weighing up to 100% of the towcar's kerbweight (see illustration B) and still perform adequately

- **NEW CARAVANNERS** should start by loading their caravan to 85% of the car's kerbweight

- The **MORE EXPERIENCED** you become, the more you will be able to judge if your outfit is behaving properly under all road conditions. At this point, decide whether you want or need to increase the weight ratio

- Even the most experienced caravanner should **NEVER TOW** a caravan that weighs more than their car (illustration C). A caravan that is heavier than the car can lead to 'the tail wagging the dog' out on the open road – an accident usually follows

⚠ WHAT WEIGHTS?

- **KERBWEIGHT** – the weight of the car, without passengers or luggage, but with a full tank of petrol. Look for this in your car's handbook or call your local dealer for information

- **MANUFACTURER'S TOWING WEIGHT** – the maximum weight that a car's manufacturer states it can tow. This may sometimes be either very conservative or over-optimistic, so work out your car's towing limit yourself, too

- **THE WEIGHT OF A FULLY LADEN** caravan must never exceed the weight it has been designed to carry by its manufacturer, whatever your car's kerbweight

Going to extremes

This outfit follows the old maxim 'buy the biggest car and the smallest caravan you can find'. The caravan is just a fraction of the towcar's weight and well within its towing capabilities. There would be no stability problems here, but not everyone can afford to buy or run a large car, and another drawback is that drivers may forget that they are actually towing anything. If this happens they could break the speed limit or cut in too early when overtaking.

The right combination

As well as the basic car to caravan weight ratio, there are other factors – power, torque, fuel type and so on – that determine whether your car will tow safely and efficiently. You also need to work out the weight of the things you take with you, plus the weight of any equipment that may have been fitted to your caravan since it left the factory.

WHAT IS MY TOWING FACTOR?

To use the graph on the right, you need to find out your car's towing factor. This is worked out on a power-to-weight basis.

1. Find out your car's kerbweight in hundredweight and its peak torque figure (see page 71) in pounds per foot

2. Now, divide your torque by your kerbside weight

3. Divide the number you get by 4. This will usually give you a figure between 1.0 and 2.0. Poor towcars have towing factors below 1.0; the best have towing factors of 2.2 and above

Remember that a car with a good towing factor may not necessarily be a heavy one, so your choice of caravan may still be restricted

- to convert kg to Cwt (hundredweight), divide the number of kg by 50.802345
- to convert Nm (Newton metres) to lb/ft, divide by 1.357

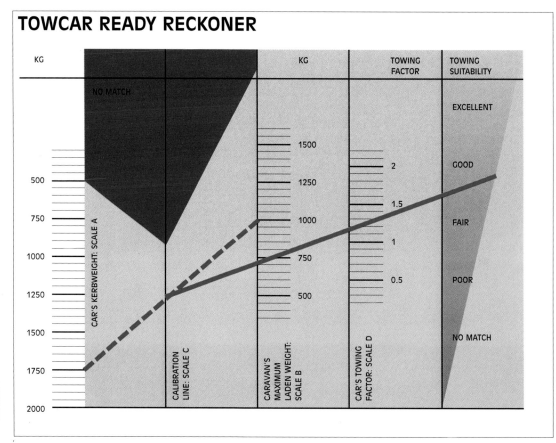

FINDING THE RIGHT RATIO

The ready-reckoner graph above uses the power-to-weight ratio of a car and the weight of a caravan to tell you if your proposed outfit is a good match.

1. Draw a line connecting the car's kerbside weight (Scale A) to the caravan's maximum laden weight (Scale B). If this line crosses the calibration line C within the red area, then the caravan/car combination is not recommended.

2. From the point where this line crosses calibration line C, draw a second line to pass through the car's towing factor (Scale D). Extend this line across to the right hand side of the graph.

3. The suitability of your car/caravan combination is now indicated. In the example shown, a car with a 1750kg kerbweight and towing factor of 1.2 is matched with a 1000kg caravan to give a good towing combination.

USED CARAVAN WEIGHTS

If you buy a used caravan that hasn't got a handbook with it, finding out its weights can prove difficult. Caravan dealers either display the weights on the caravan or are able to give them to you. With private purchases, this information can be hard to ascertain, especially if the chassis plate is missing.

Other options are to contact the manufacturer or owners' clubs. If these avenues prove fruitless, take the unladen caravan down to a weighbridge and weigh it. Then work out your allowances, load the caravan and weigh it again. You can now work out your car/caravan ratio.

Above: If you need to weigh your caravan yourself, you will have to find a public weighbridge like the one shown here and will probably be asked to pay a fee. Ensure that the weighbridge is capable of giving an accurate reading of the weight of your caravan – a fully laden lorry weighs more than a fully laden caravan.

How heavy?

As we've already discovered, it's important that you know the weight of every single item you take caravanning with you. Don't take more than your allotted loading margin or you'll exceed the maximum weight the caravan has been designed to carry. Weigh everything before your first trip out – you'll be surprised how quickly it all adds up.

Shoes weigh around 1kg a pair, boots about 2kg per pair

One person's clothes allowance for a long weekend – for example socks, underwear, 2 pairs of jeans, 2 shirts, 2 sweaters and 2 T-shirts – will weigh around 5 to 6kg

Weighing the items you intend to take is easy. As long as they are not too big or awkward, just put them on the bathroom scales

For larger items, simply stand on the bathroom scales with what you want to weigh in your arms. Take a note of the reading, subtract your own weight and you're left with the weight of the item

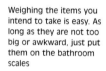

Leisure battery

One of the heaviest items you'll have to take caravanning, weighing around 15kg. The weight of a battery box (if you have one) is negligible.

Caravan step

These are generally made of plastic or (as shown here) aluminium. This keeps the weight down to around 3kg or less.

Hitchlock

This is quite heavy, but well worth making room for. A hitchlock generally weighs about 4kg.

Wheelclamp

At 15kg, this is a very weighty item. There are lighter versions but, as a rule of thumb, the lighter it is, the easier it will be for a potential thief to remove it.

Fresh water container

This version weighs around 1kg, empty. The weight of its aluminium handles, plastic filler pipe and the 12V water pump is negligible.

Pots, pans and crockery

Equipment to make and serve simple meals for a family of four will weigh around 5kg. A basic set of pans weighs about 3kg and kitchen necessities – aluminium foil, food bags, rubbish bags, kitchen roll, matches and plastic storage containers – can weigh 2 to 3kg altogether.

Bedding

Each sleeping bag or duvet weighs between 2 and 3kg. Add a sheet, duvet cover, pillow and a pillowcase and that makes another 2 to 3kg per bed.

Mains hook-up cable

Shorter, lighter cables are available, but the average length of 20 to 25m of sturdy cable (to reach the most distant hook-ups) is quite heavy, at 5kg.

Caravan jack

Another fairly weighty item, at 5kg, but again not one that should be sacrificed in order to save a bit more weight for clothes and personal effects.

Chemical toilet

The toilet itself is around 5kg, and the chemicals it needs add about another 1kg.

Gas cylinder

Look on the side of the cylinder for its weight. This is a 7kg cylinder and about the biggest one, in terms of size, that will fit into a caravan's gas locker.

Spare wheel and tyre

Together these weigh a considerable 12kg – but you really can't caravan without them.

Safe loading

After you've worked out the weight of the things you want to take with you, ensuring that this doesn't exceed the caravan's Maximum Design Weight, don't be tempted to simply put all your belongings wherever they will fit. There is an art to good loading, and where you put items – especially the heavier ones – can significantly affect your tourer's stability.

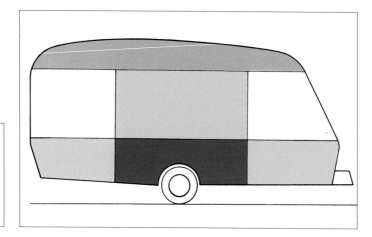

Key

■ – HEAVY ITEMS

▨ – MEDIUM-WEIGHT ITEMS

▨ – LIGHT ITEMS

Apportioning your load

This picture shows how your load should be distributed while you're on the road – heaviest items over and just in front of or just behind the axle; medium-weight items either low down and along the floor, or higher, but only over the axle area; lightest items at the top. There are two basic rules: keep the main load low and close to the axle. The lower down the stowed items, the lower the centre of gravity and the more stable your caravan will be.

Overloading at the front

Storing heavy items at the front causes the caravan to go 'nose down'. As well as affecting the noseweight and bringing it up to an unacceptable weight, it also presses down on the back of the car. This will cause damage to the car's rear suspension and, if it is front-wheel drive, take the drive wheels dangerously out of contact with the road.

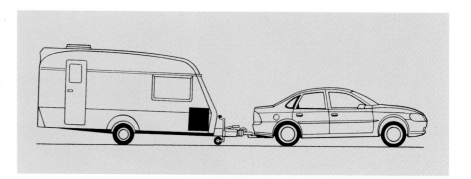

Overloading at the rear

Because a caravan is free to swing behind the towing vehicle, heavy weights at the extreme rear will multiply the pendulum effect if the caravan starts swinging. A badly distributed load can mean the difference between recovering from this situation or not being able to control the outfit and having a crash. If your caravan has a bike rack on the rear, follow the manufacturer's instructions for loading it. Loading too heavily at one side can cause instability or a tyre blow-out, so try to load both sides of your tourer evenly.

LOADING UP YOUR KITCHEN

What goes where?

The kitchen shown here, positioned in the centre of the caravan between two living 'ends', has particularly well-planned storage space. Caravans with central kitchens have well-balanced weight distribution because much of the load is positioned over the central axle area. If your kitchen is at the end of the caravan, take care, because you must watch how much you load this area. Caravanners with an end kitchen should load heavy consumables and kitchenware elsewhere in the caravan and then re-pack it into the kitchen area once on site.

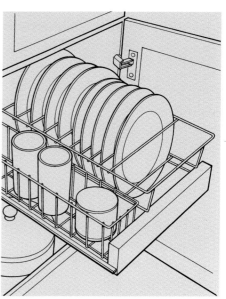

Right: The various kinds of pull-out baskets that fit inside kitchen cupboards are ideal for storing small or easily damaged items safely.

Smaller items

Small or fragile items must be stored with care – even negotiating a roundabout can cause things to bounce around. The ideal option is cupboards and drawers that are specially designed to contain these belongings safely – such as within the wire baskets shown here. Remember that tinned food should be stowed as low as possible – the weight of a moving tin may damage the wood inside a locker or cause the locker catches to burst and the tin to fall out and cause further damage.

NOSEWEIGHT

Noseweight is the maximum allowed static downward pressure (while the caravan is stationary) that can be exerted on the back of the car. Your car manufacturer's recommended noseweight will be in your handbook, or check with your local car dealer. If you have a noseweight gauge (right), place your caravan on level ground, with its steadies up, and put the gauge under the hitchhead. Lift the jockey wheel and take the reading. If you don't have a gauge, use a stick placed under the hitchhead and on top of bathroom scales.

Where it all goes

Once you appreciate how important it is for the things you take with you to be loaded safely, you will begin to see that there is usually a handy storage place for everything. Either the caravan has been designed that way, or it is simply a matter of common sense. Here are some storage ideas for the kind of equipment you are likely to take with you.

Gas cylinders, mains cable and levellers

The gas locker at the front of the caravan is designed to house your gas supply – there are special straps here that hold in the gas cylinder(s). You can also store levelling chocks in the locker. These are light and may be needed as soon as you arrive on site, so it's better if they're easy to locate. The same applies to the mains cable. Don't be tempted to put heavy items in the gas locker just because there's room – you will exceed your noseweight.

Water containers

The washroom is a handy place for your fresh and waste water containers. The containers themselves may either be wet or have mud and grass clippings stuck to them after sitting outside the caravan. Your washroom will probably have a fitted shower tray, so a quick rinse down will clean them up – much easier than trying to get mud and debris out of your caravan carpet.

Heavyweight items

Heavier items – which should be packed on the caravan floor, over the axle area (see page 62) – include barbecues and large boxes of food. This is also the place to stow your awning and poles, TV, crates of drinks and so on. Always make sure that anything packed here is secure, otherwise heavy braking may cause them to shoot forwards and damage the furniture at the front of the caravan.

Clothes care

As well as wardrobe hanging space, your tourer will usually have shelving or plastic-coated baskets for storing towels and jumpers. Keep the valuable hanging space for trousers, jackets, coats and long dresses. Put all your other, lighter clothing into roof lockers. Store shoes low down – it is not, however, always possible to keep them in the bottom of the wardrobe, as space heaters are frequently sited here.

Medium-weight items

Things such as bicycles and plastic patio furniture should be stored just in front of or behind the axle – that is, around the heavier items (see page 62). Again, pack them tightly or pack other, smaller things around them, filling the width of the caravan floor to stop them from sliding about and damaging the caravan's interior.

Locker space

Caravans always have a generous amount of roof lockers, so there will be plenty of storage space for T-shirts, shorts and summer gear. Each member of the family should be assigned their own lockers, so they are responsible for filling them up and emptying them, ensuring that nothing is left behind in the caravan at the end of each trip.

Bedding

Your bedding stows away in the bed lockers or boxes that are situated underneath the seating/sleeping areas. Access to these large storage spaces is found under the cushions, by lifting up a lid or pushing back slats. This can prove quite difficult for those of slight build, so look for drop-down access flaps at the front of the seats or, better still, pull-out basket storage.

Clever packing

You may begin to feel that you will never be able to fit in all the very differently sized, shaped and packaged objects that you want to take along. All you need, however, is a little ingenuity. There are lots of ways to save space and weight – and ensure that a tow down a bumpy lane won't send the contents of your caravan flying across its floor.

Kitchenware

This is one area where you can reduce your load considerably. Today's 'picnicware' is stylish and practical – it is much lighter than porcelain and glass equivalents and won't break easily. If you do have fragile pieces, pack them in a rack, wrapped in a tea-towel, as shown. Look for kitchen tools made from heavy-duty plastic rather than metal. It's always a good idea to buy items specifically for the caravan and to leave them, ready for use, stowed away in it. This way, you won't leave crucial items at home.

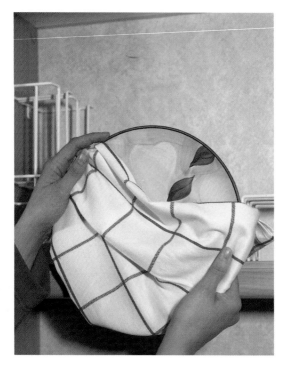

Storage racks

Most caravans have these racks fitted into the overhead kitchen lockers. They are made from either pre-formed plastic or plastic-coated wire and usually hold four plates, four mugs and four cereal bowls. Some have straps to hold crockery in place. If your tourer doesn't have a rack, you can buy one from a caravan accessory shop and fit it yourself.

Re-bagging food

Food packaged in large boxes takes up precious space and glass jars and bottles are likely to smash if they move around in cupboards. Try taking out the inner bags, or tipping the contents into handy-size freezer bags, sealed with a peg. This also means that you won't waste space taking along a week's supply if you're only going away for a weekend.

Lightweight crates

These lightweight plastic crates are perfect for storing food – they come in various sizes and fold down flat for easy storage between trips. There's nothing, however, to stop you carrying food in cardboard boxes. Select ones that fit snugly into the cupboards and cut down the front panel a little so it's easy to see what's inside and to take it out.

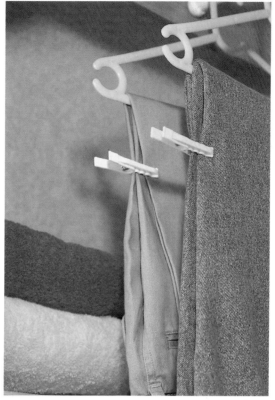

Securing clothes

You may find that the motion of the moving caravan causes trousers to slip off their hangers and end up in a pile at the bottom of the wardrobe. Prevent this by pegging them at each side, close to the hanger. Treat dresses in the same way, pegging straps just under the 'shoulders' of the hanger.

Sensible packaging

Wherever you can, save weight by taking any ready-made food in packets rather than tins. Other useful things to look out for are supermarket trial packs of household cleaners, washing-up liquid, laundry products and so on, to avoid having to find room for large, sometimes heavy, containers. A family-sized box of washing powder, for example, can weigh 3.5kg.

Avoiding spills

Of all kitchen spillages, milk is one of the worst, often leaving a nasty smell that's difficult to eradicate. Cartons of milk are only safe in the caravan fridge as long as they have not been opened. Avoid spills in the first place by putting milk, fruit juice and so on in screw-top jars or plastic screw-top beakers.

CHAPTER 5

Your
TOWCAR

There are certain important things that you should look for in a prospective towcar. As a general rule, the bigger the car, the better. However, many ordinary, modern family cars make excellent towcars and it may well be that what you're driving now will be perfectly suitable for towing. Weight-to-power ratio, transmission and body style can all affect just how well your car will tow. There are also products available that can cure sagging suspension and improve stability.

The right car, the right accessories, and using your car for valuable storage

Family towcars

Y ou may be lucky enough to have just the right car to suit the caravan you're interested in buying, or you could be weighing up the pros and cons of each type of car with a view to getting a new one. Whatever your situation, you'll probably be looking at ordinary family saloon cars. But which size of car will suit your needs – as well as your caravan's?

OVERHANG

Overhang is the distance between the car's rear axle and the towball.

In cars with **A LONG OVERHANG**, the car's rear end may be pushed down by the caravan. This will probably need suspension aids to correct it (see pages 80-81). Without these, the caravan could pitch from front to back or sway from side to side. If your car is even slightly down at the rear, your headlights will dazzle on-coming traffic, unless you have headlamp angle adjusters.
A SHORT OVERHANG puts the wheels further back, at the 'corners' of the car, which will tend to make your caravan more stable.

SMALL FAMILY CAR

Advantages

More and more small cars with impressive engine performance and excellent fuel economy are being launched every year. Go for the largest engine you can afford, so that you can take full advantage of the car's good power to weight ratio – smaller towcars often perform better than larger models fitted with the same size of engine. Remember that fuel economy always drops when you are towing a caravan, so starting off your caravanning career with a smaller-engined car will be less of a shock to your budget.

Disadvantages

A family of five, or parents with growing teenagers, may find this size of car a bit cramped – head- and legroom-wise – on the type of long journey you're likely to undertake with a caravan. The kerb weight (see page 57), which will be lighter than that of a larger car, can prove a problem when you are trying to match a caravan to the car – you may find that your choice is quite limited in comparison. The 1.6-litre vehicle shown here has a fairly good 990kg kerbweight, giving a beginner's 85% guide weight of 842kg.

TORQUE

Torque, the turning power generated by the engine, is a measure of engine performance. Look for good, 'low-down' torque (that is – good torque at low engine speeds).

THE ADDED WEIGHT of a caravan on the back means that your towcar will need quite a lot of pulling power and grip. Good pulling power will allow you to pull away easily at roundabouts and traffic lights while also cutting down the number of gear changes needed. For example, if the car's torque peaks at 6000rpm (revolutions of the engine per minute), then the biggest surge of pulling power comes when the roundabout is only visible in the rear view mirror – too late for a caravanner. If it peaks at 3600rpm, it will be much more help while you're actually accelerating over the roundabout.

CAR MANUFACTURERS usually specify the peak torque figure, and at what rpm it is produced. Most modern engines produce their maximum torque at between 2500rpm and 4000rpm.

LARGE FAMILY CAR

Advantages

This type of vehicle is the standard caravanning car and, conveniently enough, quite a few people have a company car in this category. There is plenty of headroom and legroom inside, so older children won't feel squashed. Engine sizes start where the smaller cars leave off, and cars this size in 1.8- and 2.0-litre variants generally make excellent towcars. Fuel economy will still be reasonable while towing with a car this size, which is likely to have very aerodynamic styling. Prices are keen as competition is especially fierce in this class of car.

Disadvantages

With this style of car, you will still be slightly limited in your choice of caravan. Although such a car is designed to accommodate families, caravan weights often mean that a four- or five-berth caravan to match this weight of car (the car below has a kerb weight of 1267kg) is a medium-specification one rather than a heavier, luxury model complete with all the extra equipment. If there is just the two of you and you're buying a small, two-berth caravan, then a car like this gives you the option of having a more sophisticated (and so heavier) caravan.

Think carefully about matching the right car to your caravan and to your holiday lifestyle.

Larger cars

With bigger cars, it often comes down to what your particular preferences are. You may be happy with the extra length of an estate car but not so enthusiastic about day-to-day motoring in something as large as an off-road vehicle. These car types are all capable of carrying a family of five or more in comfort.

There's a greater choice of larger cars than ever, making group or family outings a far more straightforward and comfortable proposition.

ESTATE CAR

Advantages
This is the ideal car if you've got family and pets to take along caravanning. Certain estates have long been considered the caravanners' choice, as their weight, durability and often stiffer suspension make them perfect for towing. If you are buying an estate car, look for one with a load cover. This can be pulled over items left in the boot, so that they are not on view to passers by. Your choice of caravan is widened a little if you buy an estate, as they are pretty heavy vehicles – the car shown here has a kerbweight of 1574kg.

Disadvantages
As with saloons, some estates suffer from excessive overhang and can be prone to nose-to-tail rocking while towing. If you want to take more stuff with you than your caravan loading margin dictates, don't put large piles of it in the back of the estate. It's a common misconception that this increases the car's kerbweight and so lets you load more into the caravan. This is rather like throwing several bags of cement into your car and expecting it to perform just as well. The more weight you put in the car, the more you affect performance.

PEOPLE-CARRIER

Advantages
For those with more than five in their family, a 'people-carrier' is often the only option if everyone wants to go on holiday together. This model has seven seats and lots of comfort features for families on the move, including seats that swivel to face each other, cup holders, map pockets and baggage hooks. The extra height that these vehicles have over ordinary cars is an advantage when touring on country lanes and motorways, giving the driver a clear view ahead.

POWER-TO-WEIGHT RATIO

Modern car production methods mean that one basic body shell has to cover each car in a range, from the most basic to the most sophisticated. This means that the only real difference between models is the size of the engine, and so it is this that affects your car-and-caravan's power to weight ratio. Car performance varies enormously, so make sure that you know the brake horsepower (bhp) of your engine – it's usually measured as bhp per ton. As a general guide to the minimum you should tow with in terms of weight: power, look for at least 40bhp per ton of your outfit's 'train weight'. This is the weight that the engine has to pull – the loaded car and loaded caravan.

LOOKING AFTER A TOWCAR

- **DON'T ASK TOO MUCH** of your towcar. If it is struggling up a hill, change down a gear

- **DON'T PARK** a car with a catalytic converter in long, dry grass – this can make the converter extremely hot, which might in turn ignite the grass. Remember that leaded fuel renders catalytic converters useless, as does driving through deep water and push- or tow-starting

- If you are buying a car that has **HAD A TOWBAR FITTED** to it, take it to your local car dealership to make sure that you have the right kind of towbar, and that it is fitted correctly

- Look out for **WEAR AND TEAR ON THE TOWBALL** and check that it seems to be fitting under the hitchhead properly. If in doubt, have it checked out by a professional

OFF-ROADER

Disadvantages

Buy the largest engine size you can afford to run – some of these vehicles can be slightly underpowered for their size. The styling – rather like a panel van – is quite an acquired taste. The doors have to be quite large, so some are fitted with the sliding type rather than those that open outwards. This is to make sure that passengers don't open the doors into other vehicles, but to some potential purchasers it makes the people-carrier too van-like. High sides can make them susceptible to side winds.

Advantages

Originally, this type of vehicle was produced for difficult terrain and was designed to tow things such as agricultural machinery. Today, this is the towcar that many caravanners aspire to. In its true form it is rugged, can pull the heaviest caravans with ease, will get you off particularly muddy pitches and give you an elevated road view. Turbo-charged diesel variants are common and their low-down pulling power makes them the perfect partners for caravans. Kerbside weights are around 1800kg to 2000kg.

Disadvantages

Make sure that you buy a vehicle truly designed for 'off-roading' – those under 2.5 litres or 1600kg won't do the job as well. Rather than choose one of these, buy a four wheel drive saloon. Don't expect car-like handling and cornering – these are working vehicles with a high centre of gravity. The suspension in some models can give a hard ride – as a result, caravan manufacturers may refuse to honour warranty claims. (Although you can fit a cushioning device between towbar and towball.) Another drawback is the high fuel consumption.

Towbars

Y ou can't tow a caravan until a towbar has been fitted underneath your car. Connected to this is the towball, which links your car to your tourer, and nearby are the one or two electrical sockets that link the caravan to the car's electrics. Once you have a 'hook' on your car, a whole world of trailer-towing opens up – boats, motorbikes, horseboxes – subject to weight.

TOWBAR TYPES

Face-plate towbar and towball

With this towbar type, the towball is bolted to a face-plate on the bracket by two or four high-tensile steel bolts. The main advantage of this type of fitting is that, if the towball sits too high and pushes the caravan up at the nose, a 'drop plate' can be added. This has pairs of holes at different heights drilled into it. It is sandwiched between the towball and the face-plate, and the towball is re-attached to a set of lower holes. Face-plate towballs are usually fitted along with the towbar, at a garage, and stay on the car permanently. The towbar shown here has two electrical sockets.

12N electrical socket – see opposite page

face-plate towball

face-plate

12S electrical socket – see opposite page

CHOOSING A TOWBAR

- Don't be **TEMPTED TO CUT COSTS** – your towbar is much too important

- **THE BEST TYPE** of towbar is one approved by your car's manufacturer, as it is specially designed to fit the correct mounting points. Towbars fitted to the wrong points can lead to the car body suffering fatigue or fracture

- Some of the **MAJOR TOWBAR MAKERS** produce car manufacturer-approved towbars

- **FITTING AN UNAPPROVED** towbar can invalidate your car's warranty

Towbar with detachable towball

Becoming increasingly popular, this arrangement features a towbar with a socket, into which you simply clip the towball. The towball is then easily removed when you are not towing and stored away in the car boot.

Swan-neck towbar

This type of towbar has an integral ball. The theory behind the design is that, because there is no need for the towball to be attached to another part, there is much less chance of failure at this particular point.

COVERING UP

When you have unhitched the caravan, always put the towbar cover on. This helps to keep the ball well-greased and means that anyone rummaging in the car boot and brushing against the towball won't get grease on their clothes. This type of cover is perfect for a face-plate towball. For a swan-neck or detachable version, small caps that cover just the towball itself are available.

TOWBALL CARE

Unless you have a friction stabilizer (see pages 78-79), help to reduce friction by greasing the towball from time to time. Do this by cleaning it to get rid of any dirt and then applying a layer of multi-purpose grease. You could also grease lightly under the hitchhead.

HOW ELECTRICAL SOCKETS ARE WIRED

Two-socket arrangement

Some socket arrangements, like that shown on the opposite page, feature two 7-pin sockets – a 12N (Normal) socket and a 12S (Supplementary) one.

Socket functions

The 12N socket has a black cover and runs the trailer's main road-lights. The supply goes from the relevant car circuits to the 12N socket. The 12S socket has a white or grey cover – the corresponding grey lead on the caravan plugs in here. Power comes from the car (while it's on the move) to charge the caravan battery. This allows you to use the 12V facility to keep the fridge cool while towing and works the van's reversing lights.

Relay switches

A switch called a relay should be fitted to your towcar. This stops current flowing to the fridge and the caravan battery when the engine isn't running, so that the car battery won't go flat.

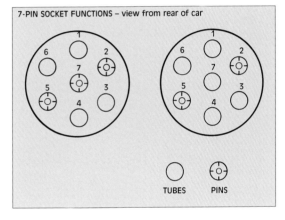

7-PIN SOCKET FUNCTIONS – view from rear of car

TUBES   PINS

12N SOCKET (ABOVE LEFT)	12S SOCKET (ABOVE RIGHT)
1 Left indicator light	1 Reversing light
2 Fog lamp	2 Auxiliary battery charging
3 Earth	3 Earth
4 Right indicator light	4 Interior lights
5 Right-hand lights	5 Sensing device
6 Brake lights	6 Fridge
7 Left-hand lights	7 Spare

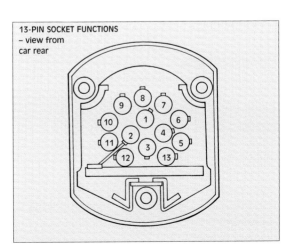

13-PIN SOCKET FUNCTIONS – view from car rear

Single-socket arrangement

Alternatively, all electrical functions may be served by one 13-pin socket on the towbar.

1 Left indicator light	8 Reversing light
2 Fog lamp	9 Auxiliary battery charging
3 Earth	10 Spare
4 Right indicator light	11 Spare
5 Right-hand lights	12 Spare
6 Brake lights	13 Earth
7 Left-hand lights	

Engine and transmission

Once you've worked out the weight issue and made a good car-to-caravan match on paper, consider the fuel your car runs on and what type of transmission it has. There are various pros and cons to towing with a petrol- or a diesel-powered car; the same is true of manual and automatic gearboxes.

MANUAL VERSUS AUTOMATIC

MANUAL TRANSMISSION
Advantages

A gearbox matches the car's speed to the speed of the engine. Torque (see page 71) is not developed evenly and so it is necessary to keep the engine speed within the range where useful torque is developed by changing gear. With a manual gearbox, you depress the clutch to disengage the drive to the wheels, and change gear. In an automatic, there is no clutch and always some slippage between the engine and the gearbox. This causes a power loss that in turn causes increased fuel consumption.

Disadvantages

With manual cars, you must change gear manually. With an automatic gearbox, you have the choice of using it purely automatically, by putting it in 'D' (Drive), or you can use the lever to select the gear required. Engaging the clutch causes a certain 'juddering', which increases wear on the car's engine, transmission and body, as well as the caravan itself. Depressing the clutch repeatedly also strains your left leg considerably — something to bear in mind if you will be stuck in holiday traffic.

DIESEL VERSUS PETROL

Although diesel can increase economy by 30-50% on petrol equivalents, the reduction in performance with standard diesel engines can be a hindrance, especially when a caravan is involved. Turbo-charging can redress the balance, although too much use of turbo will start to reverse the good fuel economy. Pre-warming (an orange light on the fascia goes out when the engine is ready to be started) and the absence of temperamental spark plugs or distributors can make starting and running easier. Service intervals for diesels may be

shorter than with petrol engines, and more regular oil changes might be needed. Other points to bear in mind:

- Diesel cars have good fuel economy. This is important when towing a caravan, which tends to increase fuel consumption through its shape and bulk

- If well-cared for, a diesel engine will manage many more miles than its petrol equivalent

- The flat torque curve of most diesels peaks at

2000-2500rpm, and so is good for towing

- Torque and bhp may be less than with petrol equivalents, so a diesel needs five well-spaced gears. Otherwise, there isn't enough stretch within the gears to reach reasonable speeds. This is why many car manufacturers fit a bigger capacity engine in their standard diesel, or add a turbo-charger

- Check the car manufacturer's towing limit. It may be lower than the petrol equivalent.

FRONT- OR REAR-WHEEL DRIVE?

Given a choice between front, rear or four-wheel drive, the car with drive to all four wheels has to be the best for better road-holding and for greater traction on muddy pitches. The majority of people, however, have to make the choice between drive to the front or drive to the rear wheels on ordinary family cars. Most cars under 2 litres in engine size are now front-wheel drive, although there are still larger cars with rear-wheel drive. Supporters of rear-wheel drive cite the fact that no amount of excess front loading of the caravan can lift the driven wheels off the road because they are at the back, but this is not an ideal safe towing scenario!

AUTOMATIC TRANSMISSION
Advantages

Pulling off with a caravan in tow – whether on the flat, on an incline or on a slippery surface – is always easier with an automatic. Power is fed to both wheels evenly (unlike some manual systems) and progressively. This means that wheel spin is less likely. Changing down a gear (for example, when you are overtaking) is faster than with a manual, as you can use the 'kickdown' method – changing gear by pressing the accelerator down sharply, allowing you to make a swift, safe manoeuvre.

Disadvantages

Automatics use around 10% more fuel than manuals. Winding around mountain passes and hot weather can cause the oil in the gearbox to heat up when towing, so a transmission cooler must usually be fitted if the car doesn't have one as standard. The anti-runback device on first gear allows you to hold your outfit momentarily on modest hills without applying the handbrake – but never use this as a real handbrake substitute in such situations, or the gearbox will overheat.

Stabilizers

A well-matched outfit should be rock steady on the road. Certain car and caravan combinations, however, are less stable than others and side winds or the 'bow waves' of passing lorries can cause problems. Help may be required in the form of a special stabilizing device – but never try to use these as a way of correcting a badly matched outfit.

STABILIZER TYPES

Stabilizers divide into two main types:

1. HITCHHEAD STABILIZERS
This type of stabilizer is designed to be fitted in place of the actual hitchhead (the coupling head). The towball must be free of grease, as these stabilizers work by gripping the ball in order to prevent swaying. They can be expensive, and there is the added cost of replacing the friction pads in the device.

Hitchhead stabilizers are equally easy to fit to either a swan-neck towball or a face-plate type. For the latter, however, a spacer between the plate and the towball may be needed. This ensures that there is enough space for the device, which often protrudes further than an ordinary hitchhead.

2. FRICTION-ARM STABILIZERS
This is the most popular form of stabilizer. It 'links' the car to the caravan via a metal arm that is mounted on a friction pad. This type of stabilizer is generally designed with the face-plate towball in mind, so you will need to buy a special adaptor bracket if you have a swan-neck or removable towbar.

With most designs, the car end of the arm fits into a socket next to the towball, and the caravan end slots into a cradle, which is fixed to the drawbar (the A-frame). Some versions have two arms instead of just one.

Al-Ko AKS
This hitchhead device uses a coating similar to that found in brake linings. In place as soon as you hitch up, its strength lies in reducing lateral instability. The version seen here has an indicator to show that the hitch is safely engaged, just like a normal hitchhead. A clearance of at least 60mm is required between the face-plate and the device.

The towball fits just under the head of these hitchhead-style stabilizers

Westfalia SSK
This hitchhead-type stabilizer, which needs some strength to secure, is also in position as soon as you hitch up. Special Teflon-coated pads in the head grip the towball, which must be grease-free. The emphasis is on controlling swaying; there is minimal effect on vertical instability or nose-to-tail pitching of the caravan.

Above: With an arm-type stabilizer, the car and caravan are hitched as normal, and then the arm is swung over and fixed into position.

This end of the stabilizer slots in just beneath the towball

Leaf spring type

This is the most popular type of friction-arm stabilizer (see also main picture). The device has a single leaf spring, with a rise of around 16cm, mounted on a friction pad. The spring resists pitching and the pad helps to stop swaying movements.

HOW STABILIZERS CAN HELP

Generally speaking, hitchhead-type stabilizers reduce a tourer's swinging action (which can lead to a snake; see pages 104-105) and arm-type stabilizers reduce both swinging and pitching. Pitching is where the caravan rocks up and down vertically, giving a hard ride to car passengers. Single-axle caravans are especially prone to pitching. Stabilizers that reduce pitching are often called 'load equalizing' stabilizers, as the link between the car and caravan has the effect of reducing any sinking effect at the hitch. This is obviously a much better way to reduce excessive noseweight than to move heavy items to the back of the caravan and, by doing so, cause an imbalance.

Stiffening suspension

Your caravan is loaded properly and you've checked your noseweight. You may still have a problem, however – the loaded caravan is pushing the back of your car down until the front wheels are almost off the ground. If your suspension system and shock absorbers are fine, then what you need is a specially designed aid to boost your car's rear suspension.

PINPOINTING THE PROBLEM

To check out whether the problem lies with your car's rear suspension or its shock absorbers, try the following. First, measure the distance from the ground to the wheel arch when you're hitched up. Compare this measurement to the workshop manual for your car or a brand-new model. A drop of 2.5cm is acceptable, but a large drop means that the spring(s) in the suspension could be tired or broken.

If you get a fair amount of pitching without the caravan on the back, then your shock absorbers may be faulty. Try 'bouncing' each corner of the car by pressing it down. If it bounces more than one-and-a-half times, you could well need new shock absorbers.

Is your outfit level?

The top illustration shows a level outfit, loaded properly, with total suspension efficiency. The outfit in the bottom illustration, despite correct loading and an acceptable noseweight, is 'tail down'. The tourer's retracted jockey wheel is almost on the ground and the front wheels of the car have only light contact with the road.

WHICH TYPE OF AID?

There are two main categories of suspension aid:

1. Various devices that have been designed to help the car's suspension along in some way.

2. Replacement shock absorbers that have additional features and/or load-bearing capabilities for towing.

SUSPENSION SYSTEM AIDS

Auxiliary steel springs

These suspension aids are added to your car's existing suspension system with a mounting kit. Kits are available for most makes of car and you will find that they are easy to use so you can fit these aids yourself. Auxiliary springs only come into play when the vehicle is loaded – in this case, coupled to the caravan.

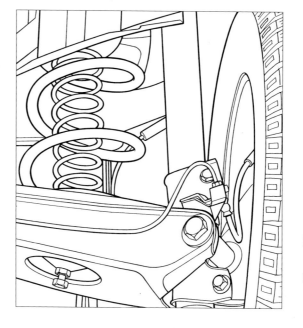

Inter-spring assisters

Suitable for any make of car, these assisters can be fitted one or two per coil (one for light loading) and are kept in place with nylon ties. The top diagram shows positioning for the greatest support, pushed to the end of the spring. The bottom diagram shows the best position to give a comfortable ride when the car is not towing the tourer.

SHOCK-ABSORBING AIDS

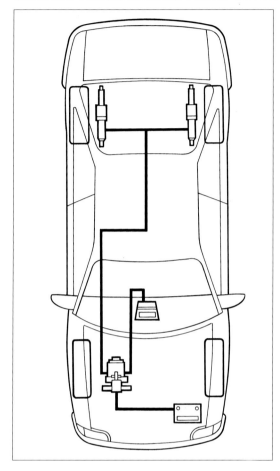

Leveller system

This is a special 'Ride-Leveller system'. It consists of a set of conventional shock absorbers with pneumatic auxiliary springs. Air pressure is increased in the system (via a dashboard control or garage compressor) to level the vehicle when it is towing and can simply be reduced afterwards.

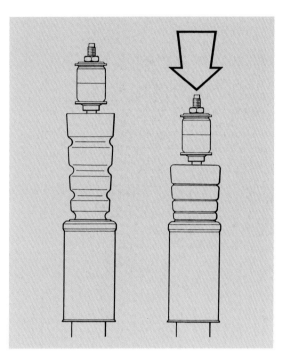

Gas-pressurized absorbers

If the car's chassis is too compact for installation of a system such as Ride-Leveller, a gas-pressurized shock absorber with a polyurethane spring can be fitted. When the vehicle is empty, the spring just touches the body of the shock absorber. When hitched up, the spring is compressed gradually and reduces sag.

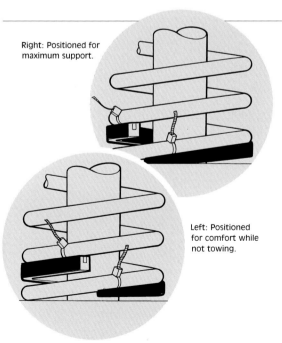

Right: Positioned for maximum support.

Left: Positioned for comfort while not towing.

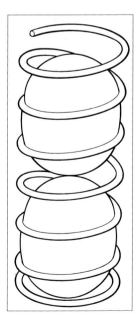

Inflatable aids

These assisters are fitted within the springs of the car's suspension system. They can also be used on cars with leaf spring suspension, if placed between the springs and chassis. Under the weight of a load, the balls are squeezed and act as a cushion, giving a more progressive action. The degree of inflation can be varied according to the load.

DON'T FORGET...

- **ALWAYS CHECK SUITABILITY** of any aid with your car's manufacturer before fitting

- Fitting some suspension stiffeners can **AFFECT THE RIDE AND HANDLING** of your car when it isn't towing, so that it feels very hard and uncomfortable

Car accessories

There will always be something extra that doesn't quite fit in any of the caravan storage areas or that has to be carried elsewhere. Your car can provide a valuable source of extra carrying space, but only if treated with respect. Watch the weight of what you are adding and where you are loading it – and always double-check that things are fixed securely.

ATTACHING A TOWBAR-MOUNTED CYCLE CARRIER

Finding the right position

1 With a carrier that fits on the towbar, as here, remove the towbar so you can fit the mounting plate. For hatchback-, boot-, or bumper-mounted carriers, fix the clips and adjust the height with the straps.

Fixing the mounting plate

2 The mounting plate for towbar-mounted carriers has two 'arms' and fits between the towball and the face-plate. It is usually secured by the bolts that fixed the towbar to the plate, or even longer ones.

Adding the carrier

3 Settle the carrier onto the mounting plate. Check that the protective cushioning is protecting the car's glass and paintwork from contact with the metal carrier.

Fix the bikes in place

4 Lift the bikes onto the arms of the carrier and strap them on. Hitch up and check that the bikes won't be banged by the front of the caravan when turning corners.

Safe solo travelling

5 Towbar-mounted bike racks are also great when you're not caravanning – but you need a light board displaying your number plate. This must be wired to or plugged into the car's circuits, as your road lights and rear plate will be obscured.

Rails and racks

In order to carry anything on top of your car, you need rails and a rack. Rails fit into tracks running the length of the roof and are purchased from car manufacturers. You can then buy adjustable racks from accessory shops that fix easily onto the rails. Some car manufacturers make special high-sided racks for vehicles such as off-roaders, with access ladders that fix to the back of the car.

Roof box

A roof box is a good place to keep all those things that don't belong in dedicated storage inside the caravan, such as outdoor games and sports equipment. Don't, however, be tempted to carry extremely heavy items in here if you have reached your caravan's Maximum Laden Weight. You will simply be hampering the car's performance (see pages 72-73).

Ski box

This type of roof box is commonly known as a 'ski' box, although it's handy for carrying equipment for any sport that has awkwardly shaped accessories – like fishing and golf. Its rounded nose and streamlined shape make it quite aerodynamic. Always remember to fix it onto your roof rails with the opening side at the edge of the car, otherwise access will be very difficult!

Carrying bikes

Putting bikes on the car roof is another alternative to carrying them on or in the caravan. It is not as easy to position bikes on this type of rack as it is on the towbar-mounted type, but the problem of direct towbar weight is avoided. As with all of these accessories, fuel consumption will rise because most of them are not particularly aerodynamic.

Ready
FOR OFF

Having bought your caravan, the exciting planning phase now begins. There's the enjoyment of deciding where to go and what to do there, as well as making sure that the caravan is in good shape and ready to tour – which you'll need to do before every trip. The pre-tour checks and hooking the caravan onto the back of your car are simple procedures, after which all that's left is to head for the open road. Form good, pre-tour habits now and they'll last you a caravanning lifetime.

Chapter 6 takes you through from planning your route to checking your lights, ready to set off

Start-of-season checks

At the beginning of every touring 'season' – whenever that is for you – there are certain checks that you can do before setting off to ensure that your caravan is ready for the road. These checks should be carried out after your caravan has had its annual professional service at an approved service centre – they are not a substitute for it.

Towbar

1 If you have a face-plate type towball, check the mounting bolts for signs of rusting, loosening or fatigue. Check a swan-neck towball for wear and tear and a detachable type to see that it is fixed securely. Lift the electrical socket covers and look for broken pins, water ingress or 'mould' (strictly speaking, corrosion deposits). Look underneath the rear of the car to check that the wiring is still connected to the electrical sockets.

Bodywork

2 Is the awning channel clear of debris and mastic? If not, your awning will be difficult to erect because its leading edge will not run through the channel easily. Check the general condition of the mastic on the trim/joins all over the caravan. Is it still soft and pliable or has it perished and gone hard? If so, you'll need to have your caravan re-sealed, something you may have to do every five years.

Caravan lights

3 Remove the lenses gently – to avoid knocking and breaking the bulbs – and clean them. Also clean any dirt or corrosion deposits off the bulb connections to ensure good contact. Check the lens seals and renew if necessary (you can buy them from your caravan dealer). Replace any blown bulbs and remember to replenish your spares stock.

Corner steadies

4 Look for signs of twisting or damage, and have steadies replaced if necessary. Grease the central screw (which runs parallel to the underside of the caravan) and put lubricant, such as general purpose oil, on the pivot points (halfway down each leg). This should keep the corner steadies operating smoothly.

Water supply

5 Take out and renew the water filter. Check the submersible pump (where fitted) for splits, perishing and discoloration around the head – replace if necessary. Now purify the water system by connecting up a fresh water container of diluted baby's bottle sterilizer or home brewing sterilizer, and opening all the taps to flush the water through. Follow this with three complete 'flushes' of pure water to take away any taste the sterilizer may have left.

Electrics and gas

6 Check that gas cylinder regulators are fitted properly, as shown. Look also to see that the grilles over the gas drop holes (see *Gas Facts* box, page 21) in the caravan floor are unobstructed. Light and check the burners; if in any doubt, have them checked by a gas service engineer. Uncoil your mains hook-up lead and inspect it for wear and loose connections. Top up your leisure battery if needed and try all taps, lights and sockets.

Sanitation

7 Clean your cassette toilet and then use water to check that it works. If it has a flush action, fill this chamber and test the mechanism. Take out the cassette and, as shown here, check the holding tank seal to make sure that it hasn't perished while the caravan has been out of use. New seals are available from caravan accessory shops.

Tyres

8 Check the tread depth, condition and pressure of your caravan tyres – and your car's, too. You should do this before every tour (see pages 134-135). If you have a spare wheel carrier fitted underneath the caravan, grease any moving parts and make sure that the nuts holding the wheel in place have not seized up due to road spray.

Route planning

Part of the enjoyment of going somewhere in your caravan is planning how to get there. Spend some time poring over maps, working out your journey time and the best route to take with your tourer. It will pay off when you arrive at the site feeling relaxed and ready to start your holiday, and not bad-tempered after a tiring, difficult drive.

Which map?

As well as choosing a map that is easy to read, guidebooks giving places to see and things to do in the area you are visiting are also well worth having.

Map reading

A bad route will add hours to your journey time. Watch out for hills, mountain passes and single-track roads – these all cause problems for caravans. If you belong to a motoring organization, call to check which routes are closed, have roadworks or are unsuitable for caravans.

Thinking ahead

At what time of year – and day – do you plan to travel? Public holidays and factory shut-down weeks will often see roads jammed to a standstill. Try to take to the larger roads – passing agricultural vehicles on country lanes is difficult while towing and annoys other road users!

Motorway services

Motorway service stations have a special area set aside for caravans – some are better than others. It is possible to pay to stay overnight at some service areas, but using gas appliances may be forbidden, due to the fire risk. Look out also for designated roadside rest areas where there are toilet facilities and where you can have a picnic and stretch your legs.

Pace yourself

Take a break every hour or so and get out of the car for a walk. If you have children, keep the journey time to a minimum, or they may go off caravanning very rapidly! Don't forget to add the time of any sea crossing on to your journey.

Above: This sign at a motorway service station means that a special caravan area is available.

Look for a large-scale map that details the entire road network – one that shows service areas and tourist attractions along the way may come in useful on a long journey.

Maps: With kind permission of Ordnance Survey Crown Copyright and Michelin Tyre plc (9601060-118).

Hitching up

Hitching up is the name given to the act of joining – or coupling – the caravan to the car so that you can go caravanning. There's nothing difficult about it and it is possible for just one person to hitch up – although it's much easier with two. Make things simpler by using the same procedure and following the safety checks every time you set out.

HOW TO COUPLE THE CARAVAN TO YOUR CAR

Preparatory checks

1 Before you start hitching up, make sure that the caravan is completely ready for the road. You will already have loaded the caravan properly and checked that your caravan's noseweight is correct. Now check that the caravan handbrake is on, the steadies are down and the caravan wheels are chocked if it is standing on a slope. That done, go inside the caravan and check once again that everything is securely loaded and that each window or roof light

is closed and fastened. All appliances should be turned off and the rocker switch on the 12V distribution panel should be in the centre – the 'off' position.

Communicating clearly

2 Hitching up is best done by two people – one to manoeuvre the car and the other to keep an eye on the hitchhead and direct the driver. Before you start, agree a system of communication with your partner so that the driver knows exactly what to do and where to go. You will need a signal for 'left' and 'right' so that the driver can manoeuvre towards the hitchhead. 'Come on' and 'stop' are the other main signals that you'll need. Stand close to the hitchhead so that you can see the towbar coming towards it and also so that the driver can see you and your hand signals absolutely clearly.

Getting into position

3 Once you are sure that everything is in order, get ready to hitch. Raise the corner steadies and wind the jockey wheel handle a few turns. This is done to lift the hitchhead so that when the car is backed towards the caravan, the hitchhead does not collide with the towball and is ready to receive it. Next, take the cover off the towball. The driver should then back towards the caravan slowly, aided by your directions. Once the car's towball is under the hitchhead (so that, from above, you cannot see the towball) then the car is in the correct position for hitching up.

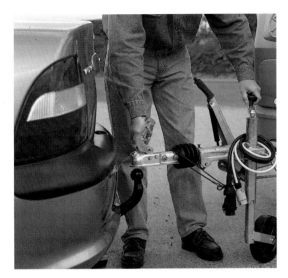

Are you hitched properly?

4 Whatever type of hitchhead you happen to have on your caravan, the principle is exactly the same. The handle on top of the head should be lifted up into its highest position and the jockey wheel should be wound back down until the head makes contact with the towball. The handle will almost drop by itself and at this point you should hear a dull 'click' as the towball is engaged by the head. You will find that modern Al-Ko hitches have a small red button at the front that pops up and shows green when the hitch is successfully connected to the towball.

Connecting up the electrics

5 Ideally, you should clip the breakaway cable to a solid part of the towbar. Many caravanners loop it around the towball neck, as shown here, although there is the possibility that the cable could come over the top if the car and caravan separate. The best securing point is a 'pig's curly tail', available from accessory shops, which can be fitted afterwards. The cable coils through this and clips back on itself. Now plug the electrical lead(s) into the car's socket(s). If the lead(s) hang near to the ground, loop it (them) into coils before plugging in, to avoid wear and damage to the wiring.

ALWAYS REMEMBER

- **FOLLOW THIS SEQUENCE** of events until it becomes second nature, and that way you won't forget any important task

- Unless they are very long (as in our pictures) **DON'T WRAP LOOSE ELECTRICAL CABLES** around the A-frame, jockey wheel handle or hitchhead. Restricting them in this way may cause them to pop out of the sockets when the caravan goes round a corner

- **CAREFULLY TWISTING** the cables to shorten them allows them to flex as you take corners. Do not hold them at the plug end and twist – you may pull the wires out of their housing

- **REMEMBER** to attach the breakaway cable

- **NEVER FORGET** to take up your corner steadies. If you leave the steadies down and try to drive off, you will bend or break them, and possibly twist the chassis

And finally...

6 Wind up the jockey wheel as far as it will go. Some wheel casings have a cut-out portion so that when the wheel is wound right up, the stays holding the wheel to the casing fit in the gap. This holds the wheel firmly in place so that it doesn't swing about and perhaps work loose while you are on the road. Undo the jockey wheel clamp and lift the casing up as far as the wheel will allow. Tighten the clamp three turns or so. Finally, take off the caravan handbrake. Don't forget to put on your towing mirrors and go through your pre-tour checks (see pages 92-93) before you set off.

Before you go

Once you have done your start-of-season maintenance there is another set of checks that you must carry out before venturing onto the road. Basically, these ensure that your caravan's road lights are working and that everything is securely stowed and ready for touring. Go through these checks after you have hitched up – in the same order each time.

TESTING YOUR CARAVAN ROAD-LIGHTS

Above: As you test your lights, your helper should stand to one side of the caravan, towards the rear, so that you can see him in your towing mirrors. Open your window so that you can also hear each other.

Checking each light in turn

1 Basically, work your way through all your car lights to check that the corresponding lights illuminate on the caravan. You will need some help to do this properly. Call out which car lights you have put on, and wait for your helper to affirm that the same ones on the caravan are working. Any lighting check must include the fog lights, brake lights and – if you have them on your caravan – your reversing lights. It must also include your direction indicators and indicator warning device (see page 93). Also check hazard flashers. Your helper must also check that the rear number plate on the caravan will illuminate clearly, as well as small marker lights near the top of the caravan, towards the front and rear. Whenever you run through your lights tests, try to do them in the same sequence every time.

Checking circuits

2 By going through this 'pre-flight' lights checklist each time you set out, you will be able to spot any bulbs that need replacing or fuses in the car that may have blown. A show of 'fairy lights' – rear lamps flashing when you try to use your indicators – could mean that there is a problem with your caravan or car's circuits, or with the electrical connections.

92

OTHER CHECKS

Indicator warning device

1 This tells you whether your car and caravan direction indicator lights are working together as they should and operates whenever you use your car indicators. The device is commonly a flashing light on your car dashboard, with a towbar symbol on it, or there may also be a beeping noise – useful in case you don't notice the flashing symbol for some reason. Most modern cars are fitted with the fascia light for this device as standard (wiring can then be done later at a garage).

General connections

2 It's worth checking the hitch point carefully once again. Make sure that you have taken the caravan handbrake all the way off and that the jockey wheel is wound up to its full extent and clamped firmly in its travelling position. Have another look to see that the breakaway cable is attached – and to the correct fixing point. Finally, your electrical connections should be firmly in their sockets, with no wires dangling down.

⚠ ON-ROAD CHECKS

- Once you have gone a little way **DOWN THE ROAD**, it's always a good idea to pull into a lay-by and make sure that everything is still working well
- You should **LOOK THROUGH THE CARAVAN WINDOWS** to check that no lockers have come open and discharged their contents. Are all interior doors still fastened shut?
- Is the **HEAVY GEAR OVER THE AXLE** still tightly packed?
- Are the **ROOF VENTS STILL DOWN AND THE WINDOWS CLOSED** and fastened?
- Are the **CARAVAN TYRES** unnecessarily hot after such a short journey?

Towing mirrors

3 Now adjust your towing mirrors. Do the one on the driver's side yourself and direct your partner to adjust the one on the passenger side of the car.

Caravan interior

4 Finally, check that everything inside your tourer is securely stowed away, and unlikely to burst out of cupboards and lockers. Make sure that all doors, windows and roof vents are securely fastened. If not, doors could keep banging open and shut and might get damaged and open windows or roof-lights could rip off at high speeds.

CHAPTER 7

Towing a CARAVAN

If the prospect of towing concerns you, try viewing the situation from this angle – whatever car you're driving simply gets a little bigger when your caravan is hitched up. Thinking in these terms, you'll find that you naturally adjust your driving style to accommodate the length, width and weight of your caravan. Reversing around corners and turning in tight spots can be a little trickier, but it needn't be a major problem. Follow a few basic rules and you'll soon wonder why you ever had any worries.

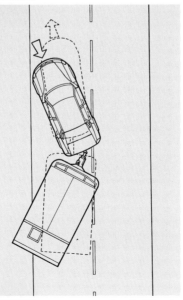

Learn how to handle different manoeuvres and spot potentially difficult situations

Out on the road

Taking to the open road with your holiday home behind you for the first time is exciting – don't let yourself feel daunted. It's simply a question of driving something bigger, so think about the extra width and length and allow for it. Just like when you first started driving a car, you'll soon get a feel for this new vehicle.

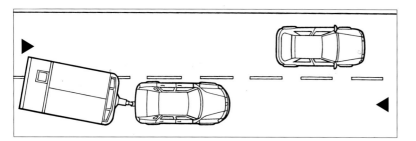

Overtaking moving objects

1 You will have to pass other traffic, cyclists, joggers, people on horseback and so on out on the road. Remember the extra width of the caravan and don't drive too close – this frightens animals and makes a collision more likely. Anticipate when you will have to overtake and pull out in good time, further out than when driving without a caravan.

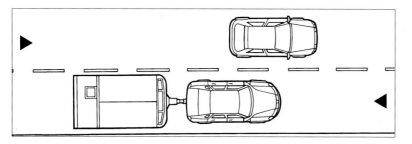

2 Pass in a straight line, a safe distance away. Leave yourself plenty of room to get back in smoothly before oncoming traffic draws near, using your towing mirrors to check that you have left enough room between the object you are passing and the back of the caravan.

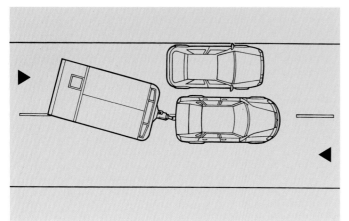

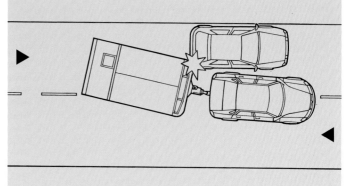

Hazards when overtaking stationary objects

1 If you have to pass a stationary object such as a parked car, then give yourself plenty of room to pull out and overtake in a straight line, as shown here. Again, you may have to pull out quite far to do this – perhaps right over the white line in the middle of the road.

2 This is what usually happens when you don't pull out early enough. The caravan is much too close to the parked car and so, as the towcar pulls out, the caravan hits the outside corner of the car.

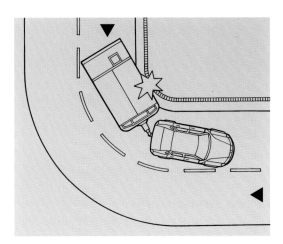

Take care when cornering

1 A towed object will always undercut the tracks left by its towing vehicle, which is why you often see lorry trailers mounting kerbs on tight street corners. If you have enough room to pull wider than usual to take a tight corner, then do so — scraping the kerb or bouncing over it is not good for your caravan's tyres. It can also be a serious threat to pedestrians standing on that corner.

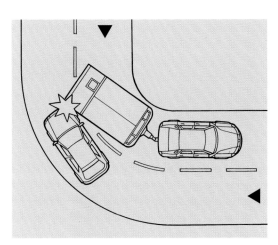

2 Don't, however, go to the opposite extreme and pull out too far. You are then in danger of the caravan crossing the white line and the back end of it clipping the corner of an oncoming car as you round the corner. Follow this advice for roundabouts too, especially mini ones, which can be difficult to negotiate without mounting the island or causing the rear end of the caravan to collide with nearby traffic.

BREAKDOWN AND RECOVERY

Don't forget to take out a breakdown and recovery policy on your caravan as well as your car. If companies know that you are towing and your car isn't instantly repairable, they can send out a recovery vehicle that can cope with both a car and a caravan.

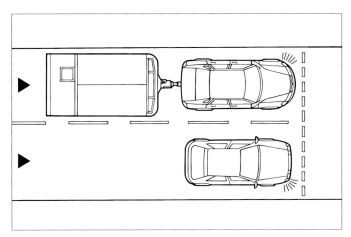

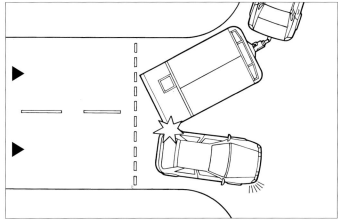

Beware at junctions

1 If you are about to turn one way and there are adjacent lanes for turning the opposite way, beware of any close vehicles. If you are at a junction and there are other lanes beside you with traffic going the same way, remember that the caravan can 'undercut' (see above), and stick to your lane.

2 Take your time in negotiating the turn. Let adjacent traffic peel off quickly and then use your towing mirrors to watch the back end of the caravan in relation to other traffic. If you take the turn too quickly, you may not be able to anticipate possible problems.

Up and down hills

Tackling steep hills simply takes common sense and an understanding of your towcar's capabilities, so everybody should be able to cope. Learn about the possible pitfalls in advance and you will find that you can bypass most difficulties.

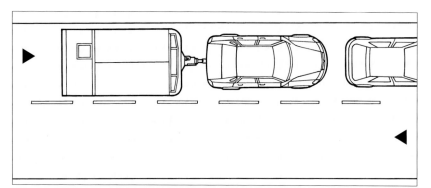

Pulling away on a hill

1 Try to avoid rush hours and busy roads – your journey should be a pleasant part of the caravanning experience. If you have manual gear change, you will generally notice your clutch slipping more when you try to pull off on a hill if you are crawling in traffic. Too few revs and you may stall the engine; too many and you may spin the wheels.

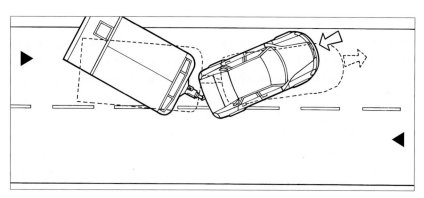

2 If you find yourself in this situation, get out of your car and tell any drivers behind about your intentions. Then reverse the caravan into the kerb at an angle and try to pull off from there. The angled approach works because the weight is not directly behind the car in this position. This means that, when the handbrake is released, the car is able to make some forward movement before the full weight of the caravan comes round behind it.

When a hill is just too steep...

Get into the habit of anticipating possible problems when you are towing. One of the main things to look out for are very steep hills. The best piece of advice here is to avoid them altogether – usually you will be able to see that one is coming up ahead. If, however, you do find yourself on a slope that your outfit can't handle, do not try to turn your caravan around yourself, to go back down the hill. This is the time to call out a breakdown and recovery service.

Right: No matter how well-matched your outfit is, very steep hills could get you into serious trouble.

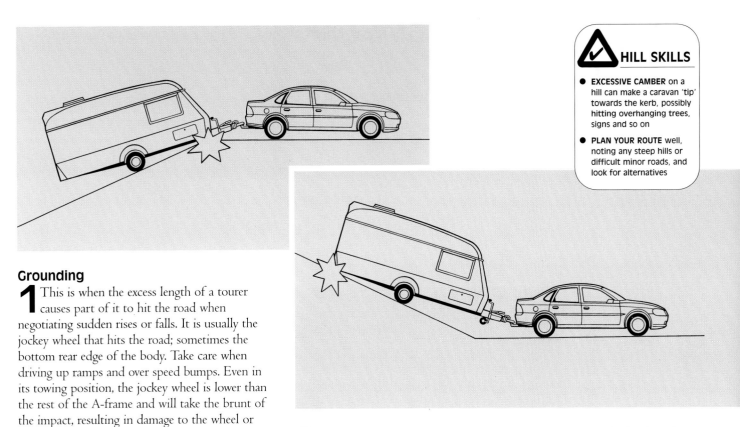

Grounding

1 This is when the excess length of a tourer causes part of it to hit the road when negotiating sudden rises or falls. It is usually the jockey wheel that hits the road; sometimes the bottom rear edge of the body. Take care when driving up ramps and over speed bumps. Even in its towing position, the jockey wheel is lower than the rest of the A-frame and will take the brunt of the impact, resulting in damage to the wheel or clamp. If you have a stabilizer fitted that sits just under the level of the A-frame, this too can be vulnerable. If you become grounded when going uphill, take out your timber levelling blocks (see page 113) and drive/reverse the car or caravan wheels onto them to raise the outfit. Once the outfit is raised, this will give you clearance.

2 Coming down a ramp can also cause grounding. If in any doubt, slow down and ask a passenger to stand to one side at the rear, giving you 'OK' or 'stop' signals. The worst scenario is that the bottom of the caravan grounds and then drags for some distance, causing serious damage to the rear of the body. If your caravan is prone to grounding at the front, check its noseweight – and your car's suspension. Should grounding occur when you are going downhill: place wooden blocks to the rear of the caravan wheels and reverse the caravan onto them. Once elevated, use every block available to maintain the height while the caravan is tentatively towed down the slope.

THE HEAVY VEHICLE EFFECT

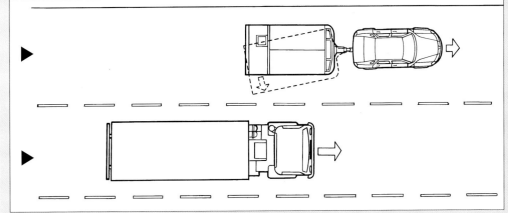

Out on the motorway, you will sometimes feel the caravan move 'in and out' as a high-sided vehicle overtakes – especially when going downhill. The height of the passing vehicle causes changes in air pressure, firstly 'sucking' the caravan towards it and then 'blowing' it back towards the car as it finally passes. Don't try to correct this – the movements are actually very slight and the caravan is in no danger of hitting the other vehicle, as long as your outfit is well-matched.

Straight-line reversing

Reversing a caravan is another skill that might seem impossible to master – but, once again, it can be perfectly straightforward. It's easy to reverse a car in a straight line but with a trailer behind you there is a new set of rules to use. Once you understand these, you should have no problems at all.

Right: Steps 1 and 2 of reversing in a straight line. 1. Start going back straight, with your steering wheel level. 2. Start to steer slightly to the left if the caravan veers in that direction.

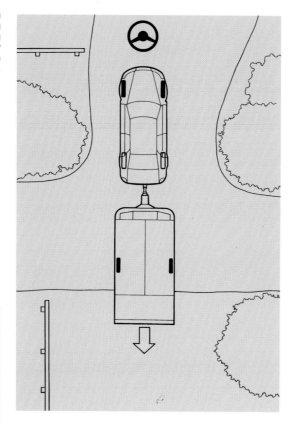

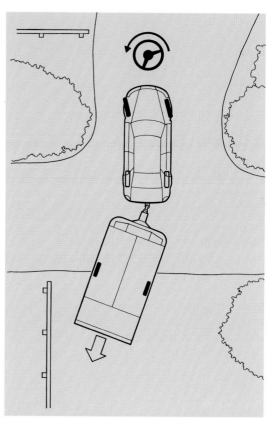

THE THEORY

It may seem a difficult concept to grasp at first, but instead of being able to turn your car steering in the direction that you want your caravan to go, you must turn it in the OPPOSITE direction.

Because this is completely different to the way in which you manoeuvre a car when there is no caravan on the back, it will take you some time and a little practice to get the angle of manoeuvring correct. This is especially critical when it comes to reversing around corners (see pages 102-103). When reversing in a straight line, the easiest way to remember what to do is to tell yourself to steer towards the towing mirror in which the caravan appears.

Start out straight

1 Straight-line reversing onto a pitch is a vital skill, and one that you can master easily if you adopt the right techniques from the start. It's a good idea for a passenger to step out of the car and stand in their communicating position to the rear and side of the caravan. Then look for objects such as low posts, walls, children's bicycles and so on, which may be in your way and which you cannot see. Start reversing as you would normally, with your steering wheel straight.

Veering one way...

2 Check each extension mirror in turn. If you see the back end of the caravan appearing in one of them, this means that the caravan is starting to veer, and you need to correct it to stop it going further in that direction. Here, the caravan has appeared in the left-hand extension mirror. To straighten up, steer smoothly towards the mirror in which the caravan appears (left), very slightly, and it will disappear.

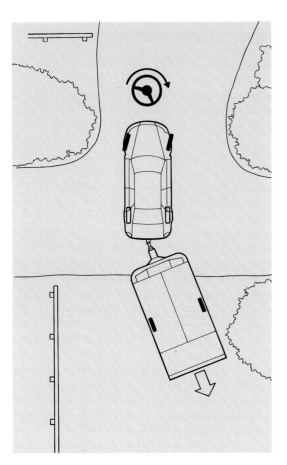

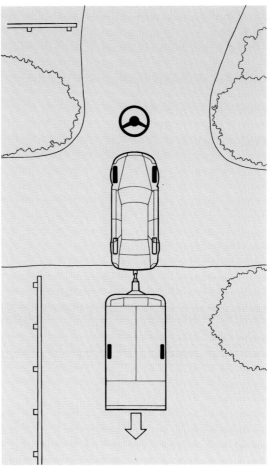

Left: Steps 3 and 4 of reversing in a straight line. 3. If your caravan appears in the other mirror, correct this by steering towards it. 4. You should now be going back in a straight line.

...and then the other

3 Now start checking each mirror in turn once again and you will probably find that, however carefully you undertook your correction, the caravan has appeared in the other mirror. Here the caravan is in the right-hand mirror and so the steering wheel is being turned very slightly to the right to correct the movement. Remember to keep your steering movements smooth and gentle.

Back on the straight

4 If you've corrected properly, you should now be reversing in a straight line. Once you have practised reversing in this way a few times you will know when and how to correct the slightest movement. If you need to build up your confidence, go to a large open area such as a supermarket car park or old airfield, and practise. Remember, take your time, look carefully in the mirrors and make your corrections smoothly, in plenty of time.

⚠️✔ SUCCESSFUL REVERSING

- **REMEMBER**, it's just a case of 'look and steer to correct' – there is no secret formula
- **CORRECT LITTLE BUT OFTEN** to keep a smooth rearward progression
- **DON'T BE PUT OFF** by your new neighbours watching you reversing onto your pitch – they're probably not giving you marks out of 10!
- **A HELPER STANDING** to the rear of the caravan but in view of your mirrors will be able to let you know about obstacles that you can't see yourself
- **PRACTISE** wherever and whenever you can – this will help you gain in skill and confidence

EFFECTIVE CORRECTION

If you steer too sharply in order to correct the movement of the caravan, it will simply disappear out of one mirror and appear immediately in the other. This will leave you constantly correcting and your car waggling from side to side – hardly a smooth progression.

If you do oversteer or don't correct in time, stop and pull forwards a couple of metres to straighten out the outfit, and then start again.

Reversing round corners

Once you have mastered straight-line reversing, you will have enough skill and feel for your caravan to enable you to reverse around corners without too much trouble. You will probably not have to do this type of reversing very often, but you never know when a good working knowledge of the procedure will come in useful.

Right: Step 1 of reversing around a corner. Start to reverse by going back straight.

Right: Step 2 of reversing around a corner. Steer to the right so that you begin to push the caravan to the left.

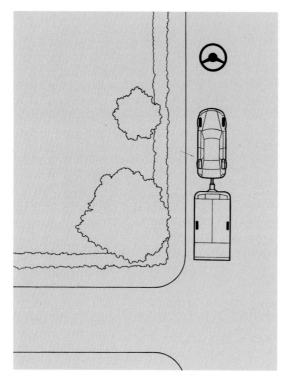

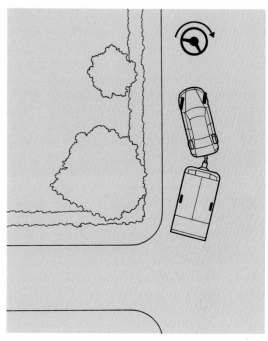

Take it slowly

1 As with reversing in a straight line, you may need a helper to keep an eye on things behind as you go back. Don't go any faster than walking pace – so that you can anticipate and correct any mistakes early on. And don't expect to be able to turn the wheel and watch the caravan go round the corner in one smooth movement. To reverse round a left-hand corner (shown here), keep your car and caravan aligned as you start to go back straight, and then turn your steering wheel to the right.

Starting to turn

2 As you reverse and slowly turn the steering wheel to the right, the car's wheels also move to the right and the car pushes the caravan round to the left, as it starts to take the corner. Keep looking ahead and in your mirrors as the car starts to swing out, as you would when reversing normally, and be prepared to stop at any time in order to let any other traffic pass safely.

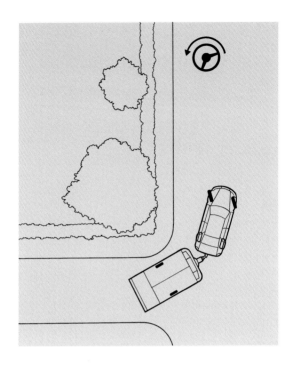

Going round

3 Once the caravan has started to turn round the corner, change the direction of the steering wheel and turn it to the left, too. This will keep the caravan going round the corner in a smooth arc.

Left: Step 3. Start steering towards the left.

Going in too tight

4 If the caravan appears to be cornering too sharply, correct the movement by steering back to the right a little, carefully. Don't make a large steering wheel turn at this point to try and compensate — this will probably only make things worse.

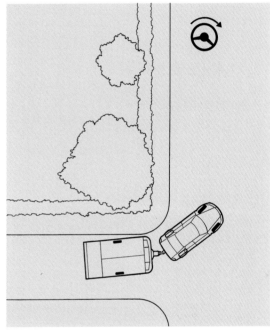

Left: Step 4. Keep going round the corner smoothly, steering a little to the right to correct if necessary.

Avoiding a jackknife

5 If it is too late, and the caravan has already cornered too sharply, then stop. If you don't, the caravan may 'jackknife' and the front edge of the caravan could come into contact with the back of the car, causing damage. If you are in a potential jackknife situation, stop and pull forwards a few metres until the outfit is straight. Then try again.

To reverse around a right-hand corner, simply follow the opposite procedure. You will also have the benefit of being able to look out of your side window when reversing round a right-hand corner.

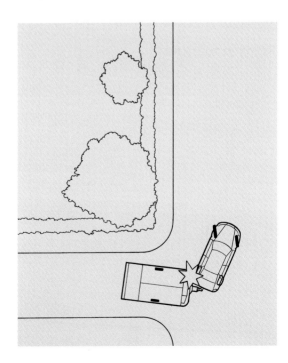

Left: Step 5. If it's too late to correct some sharp cornering, then stop the car rather than cause a jackknife situation.

Understanding snaking

Snaking, where the caravan sways from side to side, can be caused by various things – bad loading, heavy crosswinds, the bow wave from overtaking lorries, a tyre blow-out, or a combination of these factors. If you spot the signs and take action early on, snaking can be controlled. Taking the wrong action too late could lead to a serious accident.

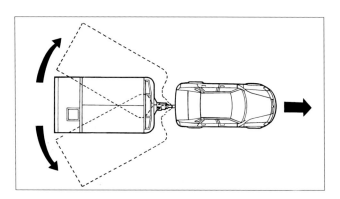

What is snaking?

You will know when you are really snaking because what starts as a gentle swaying from side to side at the rear of the caravan builds, sometimes quite suddenly, into a fierce pendulum effect. The rear of the caravan swerves from side to side so strongly that what usually happens is that the car loses control and is swung across the road by the movement of the caravan. This is known as 'the tail wagging the dog'. Badly snaking outfits usually come to rest on embankments or against central reservations with damage to both car and caravan. Sometimes, the trailer may even turn over.

HOW CAN YOU CONTROL A SNAKE?

What you shouldn't do

1 Don't try to slam on the car's brakes – you will cause an accident if you try to stop a violent snaking movement dead. As a rule, you shouldn't try to accelerate out of a snake – if you are going downhill, this will only make matters much worse (although it may help in one particular situation, see *Going Uphill*, opposite). Don't try to steer out of it – again, you'll just exacerbate the problem.

Above: **DON'T** try to steer out of the snake or slam on the brakes. Very light braking, however, may help, especially with automatic cars.

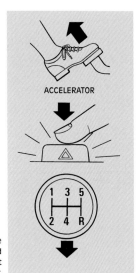

ACCELERATOR

Right: **DO** ease off on the accelerator; put on your hazard flashers; change down at least one gear.

What you should do

2 Hold the steering wheel lightly and allow some movement. Then take your foot off the accelerator so your speed starts to drop. If you have deccelerated and the caravan is still swaying, don't panic. The next step is to warn other road users that you are having difficulties – by putting on your hazard flashers so that they know to keep away – so that you can concentrate on stopping the snake. Once the car has started to slow down, try changing down one or more gears to slow it down further without using the footbrake.

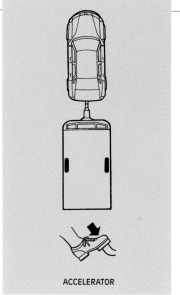

ACCELERATOR

Above: When the snake has passed, you can put your foot back on the accelerator and drive on safely.

Once you're back in control...

3 When you have the snake under control, switch off your hazard lights and drive on until you can pull over. Try to discover the cause of the snake.

SITUATIONS TO LOOK OUT FOR

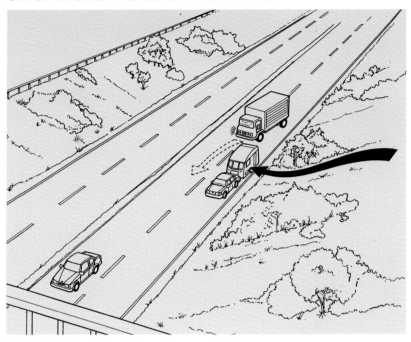

Common danger areas

Learn to spot the types of scenarios that might lead to problems – even a very well-matched and well-loaded outfit may be prone to snaking in certain situations. Harder-to-spot situations include barely visible road undulations caused by heavy traffic, but usually the signs are more obvious. The following situation contains a collection of factors that should ring alarm bells with any caravanner. Your outfit is on a motorway. The banks are not particularly steep and there is a heavy crosswind. High-sided vehicles are likely to overtake and the motorway is just starting a long downhill stretch into an open valley. Never approach a situation like this at speed. Cut your speed accordingly and use your gears to let the engine slow you down gradually.

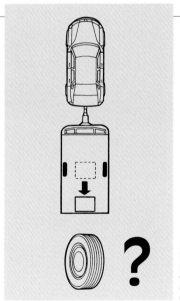

Left: A load that has moved position or a damaged tyre are common causes of snakes.

Assessing the causes

4 As you try to determine the cause, check whether your caravan tyres look healthy, or you've had a blow-out. Open the caravan door and check your load. Has anything moved significantly and caused the caravan to start swinging? Make a note of what the conditions were like where your snake took place (see *Situations To Look Out For*, above).

Lorries passing downhill

The reason that lorries passing downhill are a bad sign is as follows. Lorries passing closely at speed can have a 'suck, blow' effect on caravans (see page 99) and, if you are towing downhill, this can lead to snaking. Each time you tow uphill, the car is pulling the caravan; when towing downhill, the caravan is trying to 'pass' the car, creating a mini suck, blow effect. If a lorry then passes you, the effect gets exaggerated and may cause snaking. If this is happening when you are out on the motorway, pull over before the lorry passes so that you are driving with your kerbside wheels on the hard shoulder. This puts a distance between your outfit and the lorry and so breaks the effect.

Going uphill

You should always follow the procedure shown under *How Can You Control a Snake?*, with one exception. The only time you could possibly accelerate out of a snake is as follows. If you start to snake when coming down into a dip, you could try accelerating out of it just as you are about to climb up the other side. As you start to climb, the car will again be in control of the caravan and the snake will stop. If you are some distance from the hill when you start snaking, don't accelerate – follow normal procedure.

SNAKE CHECKLIST

- If you get into a snake, **FOLLOW THE PROCEDURE** outlined on these pages to control it

- The most important thing to remember is, when you **FEEL THE FIRST TWITCHES** of a snake, slow down. An increase in speed will make matters worse; remaining at the same speed will allow the snake to develop

- Once **THE SNAKE IS UNDER CONTROL**, determine its cause so that you can avoid the same situation in future

CHAPTER 8

Life
ON SITE

Staying on a caravan park can give you all the benefits and amenities of a hotel – swimming pools, bars, restaurants, children's play areas, tourist information, evening entertainment – or all the tranquillity of being in a peaceful spot, miles from anywhere. Once you get to the park, all you have to do is pick your pitch and set up your caravan, ready for living in. Then you can relax and get fully acquainted with what the park and the surrounding area have to offer.

This chapter covers everything from pitching your caravan to buying your daily paper on site

What do sites offer?

In the early days of caravanning you could stop wherever you were at the end of a day's journey and bed down. 'Wild camping' has became illegal in much of Europe, and special caravan parks grew up from the 1950s onwards. Site facilities differ greatly. Some are free, others aren't, and actual costs vary from one site to another.

Below: More and more sites are offering a wide range of absorbing activities for children.

Above: Site shops vary enormously in what they offer, although they can be rather expensive, so you may not want to rely on them too much.

Right: Pleasant washroom facilities can make a family holiday much more convenient and comfortable.

Picking a site

Some caravanners like to get away from it all or go somewhere to take part in a specific sport or pastime. Sites with the bare minimum of amenities suit this type of caravanner. Those with families tend to favour larger parks with plenty of facilities to alleviate boredom if the weather turns sour. The following rundown gives you an idea of what's on offer at different sites, and what you might have to pay for.

Hot showers and toilets

All commercial sites offer toilet and washing facilities. Normally, the only places without these are tiny sites for around five caravans or less – on farms or in land behind pubs, for example – and forest sites in National Parks. Showers are usually free, but may be charged on a pay-as-you-use basis via a coin box. Toilets and wash-basins with hot water are always free, and are usually housed along with the shower rooms.

Washing and drying clothes

Many parks have a laundry room, usually in the main amenity block, which provides at least deep sinks with hot and cold water for hand-washing. There are also launderette facilities at many parks, which cost a similar amount to any other launderette, while some offer outside areas for hanging washing out to dry. Ironing boards are provided free, but there may be a small charge for the use of the iron.

Shopping on site

On smaller sites, on-site shopping is usually limited to essentials such as bread, milk and eggs. As the sites get larger, so do their on-site shops. The biggest parks have mini-supermarkets stocking magazines, wines and spirits, caravan spares and gifts as well as food. They may have take-away outlets or even small restaurants. On-site pubs or clubhouses frequently offer a range of bar snacks.

Entertainment

Free entertainment – such as live bands, cabaret, talent competitions or discos – is usually laid on each night during the summer season by the bigger, holiday-centre type of site. So, if all you want is a quiet drink in the evenings, look for a smaller, less commercial site. Other entertainment facilities can include swimming pools, children's playgrounds, TV rooms, indoor games, pony trekking and a clubhouse. The provision of children's clubs is becoming more widespread, with qualified leaders taking children off their parents' hands for a few hours each day to enjoy activities such as treasure hunts, face-painting and nature walks, all within the confines of the caravan park.

Paying for your pitch

Regardless of the level of facilities on a site, the most important basic is your pitch – the space that you and your caravan occupy. Even on a site that has no other facilities to charge for, there will be a pitch fee. On some larger sites a set pitch fee will probably cover the car, caravan and all occupants, however many there are.

Extra charges

On other sites, the pitch fee may include a set number of people, and any extra people will be charged separately. Other charges are usually levied for dogs and extra cars – if friends and family come to visit you.

You are also likely to be charged extra for your awning and for a mains hook-up. As the hook-up fee is a one-off charge, and the electricity is not normally metered, many caravanners use the mains facility to its full extent, to save using their leisure battery or gas.

SEASONAL PITCHES

If you find a site you really like and keep heading back to it, ask about a seasonal pitch. With this set-up, you take the caravan to the site when it opens at the start of the year and pitch it on an agreed spot, where it stays for the rest of the time the site is open. You can then use it whenever you want. Some sites offer winter storage of caravans when they are not in use – your caravan is towed into place for your use by the site and then returned to secure storage once you have left (see also pages 142-143).

HOW DO I PICK A SITE?

- The **MAIN SOURCES OF SITES** are the annual guides sold in bookshops – such as Alan Rogers' *Good Camps Guides* – and the monthly guides found in caravan magazines. Good guides have site descriptions or symbols to indicate available facilities

- Choose guides where **INSPECTORS HAVE BEEN TO THE SITES**, or listen to others' recommendations

- **IF YOU ARE GOING AWAY IN HIGH SEASON**, call the site to book a pitch. This also gives you a chance to ask more about the site

- **QUESTIONS TO ASK:** How large is the park? How level and well-drained are the pitches and are they easily accessible? How near is the site to a busy road, railway line or airport? You don't want sleepless nights or children playing near traffic. Can you pitch where you like? Are barbecues allowed? Are there any restaurants nearby? How far is it from local attractions, such as a good beach? Note that the better guides should tell you much of this

- **DOG-OWNERS** must check first that dogs are allowed. Alan Rogers' guides, for example, list sites that don't welcome dogs

Choosing a pitch

After you have arrived on site and checked in at reception, you will either be assigned a numbered pitch or you will be left to your own devices. The latter is more usual, and you should then either drive around the site slowly to locate the best of the vacant pitches, or park your car and caravan, lock up and go off on foot to choose your spot.

Below: Pitching close to the facilities.

Right: Pitching in a dip.

Pitching close to facilities

A pitch close to the amenities – toilets, showers and laundry – is invaluable if you don't have on-board facilities, have difficulty walking very far or use a wheelchair. It is also handy if you have a chemical toilet, as the emptying point is usually located in or close to the amenity block. This pitch is especially welcome in colder weather – look for an amenity block with central heating if you will be touring in very chilly conditions. Two disadvantages of this position are that it won't be particularly peaceful, with people coming and going, and the amenity block may start to smell in warmer weather. If you would like a pitch close to an amenity block, request this when you book – most site-owners will do their best to accommodate your wishes.

Left: Under-tree pitches may seem an attractive option, but they can have various disadvantages.

THE GOOD AND THE BAD

- if you find that the **SITE ISN'T SUITABLE** in some way, you might want to look for another to move on to, so remember to take your site guide on holiday with you

- If you **REALLY ENJOY YOUR STAY** on the site you've chosen but want to try visiting a different area next time, find out from your guide whether the site you are on belongs to a group or chain in which all members have the same standards and levels of facilities

Pitching in a dip

Although pitching at the bottom of a dip or slope may give you some protection from the elements and a certain degree of seclusion, make sure you take a note of the weather forecast before doing this. Heavy rain will collect at the bottom of your dip and create a bog – causing the caravan to become uneven as its legs sink into the soft ground and a great deal of mud to be trampled into your carpet. Look at the overall lie of the land carefully. You may not notice a definite dip, but the land may be sloping down gently to where you are pitched. If there are no other caravans pitched in the corner of the site that you've just chosen, this may be a sign of damp ground. If you know that a site is prone to damp, or you are touring during a particularly wet season, ask for a hard standing when booking. These pitches have a surfaced or gravelled top to them to prevent caravans sinking into soft ground.

Pitching under trees

A nice, shady spot under a tree may have a strong appeal, especially if you are caravanning in a very hot climate. But there are disadvantages. When it rains, droplets will still be drumming down onto the roof of the caravan long after the shower has stopped, as the last of the water drips off the tree. Even if you are in a dry climate, twigs, branches, seed pods, fruit and so on are likely to fall down onto your caravan roof – possibly damaging or scratching it – if there is a high wind. Sap from certain trees is quite sticky, and letting this type of sap settle on your caravan roof may mean a lot of hard cleaning once you get home. Passing birds and squirrels also like to run around on caravan roofs – a practice that can be highly unsociable very early in the morning.

Perfect pitching

Arriving on site is an exciting experience, however many times you've done it before. If this is your first visit to the park, what is it going to be like? Whereabouts is your pitch situated? What facilities are on offer? Get everything off to the right start by following a sensible pitching and unhitching procedure – every time you reach your chosen site.

Book in at reception

1 When you pull into the entrance to the site, follow signs for reception. Don't be tempted to go straight onto the park and pitch your caravan, especially if you haven't pre-booked. Some pitches may not be in use, or may be reserved. Most sites have a long bay in front of reception where new arrivals can park, or at least plenty of room for you to pull your outfit over without blocking anybody's way on or off the site while you are booking in.

Reverse onto the pitch

2 Once you have chosen, or been allocated, your pitch, drive onto the site and locate it – the number may be on a peg or sign at the back of the pitch. Pull past your pitch and ask a passenger to get out of the car, stand towards the back and to one side of the caravan, and help you reverse onto your spot using 'OK' and 'stop' signals. If there is a wall or hedge at the rear of the pitch, allow enough room at the back for you to put the waste water container into place and open rear windows easily.

Lower the jockey wheel

3 Once you are in a good position, apply the car's handbrake and turn off the engine. You are now ready to start pitching the caravan. First, apply the caravan handbrake and then undo the jockey wheel clamp and allow the jockey wheel to descend to the floor. Now re-tighten the jockey wheel clamp.

Uncouple the connections

4 What you need to do now is to free the car so that it can be parked out of the way on your pitch, next to the caravan. The first step is to uncouple the connections between car and caravan – the breakaway cable and electrical connections (see left). Always disconnect the breakaway cable first so that you don't forget it. If you unhitch the caravan totally and leave this cable around the towbar, it will do just what it's meant to do – pull on the caravan's brakes and then snap. This will leave you with no safety breakaway cable for the journey home. Twist the electrical connection(s) slightly to free the plug(s) from the socket(s).

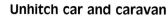

Unhitch car and caravan

5 The breakaway cable should be looped out of the way over the hitchhead and the electrical cable(s) pushed into their storage places on the A-frame (if your caravan has these), to stop water getting into the pins. Now lift the hitchhead handle and wind down the jockey wheel until it touches the ground and the towball is free of the hitchhead. Then clamp the jockey wheel into position. The driver should then pull forwards so that the cover can be replaced to protect the towball from the elements – until you need to hitch up again.

Level the caravan

6 The caravan is now likely to be 'nose up'. To level it from nose to tail, wind up the jockey wheel handle a few turns at a time while getting a helper to stand some distance away, ready to tell you whether the caravan is level. Get your helper to look at the caravan from the rear as well – if it is down at one side it will need to be levelled with ramps (see pages 114-115). Now wind down the corner steadies – remember that they must not be used to level the caravan, or chassis damage may result. If one steady is in a dip and, fully extended, does not reach the ground, use wooden blocks to fill in the 'gap' (see box).

PITCHING GUIDE

- When backing onto your pitch, **MAKE SURE YOU HAVE A HELPER** to warn you about walls, low-lying objects or passers-by

- **APPLY THE CARAVAN HANDBRAKE** to stop the caravan from rolling away while you are unhitching

- Always **REMOVE THE BREAKAWAY CABLE** before pulling forwards

- **LEVEL YOUR CARAVAN** (if it needs it) to ensure greater comfort and convenience (see *Why Level?* box on page 114)

- **WOODEN BLOCKS** make ideal levellers. Buy wood and cut it into blocks about 25cm square and 5cm thick with a handsaw

Getting level

A level caravan makes life on site much more comfortable and convenient. After you have pitched and the caravan is level from end to end, look at it from the front or from behind. If it leans to one side, this is the side you will now need to level. Below you can see the different types of device available for levelling a caravan from side to side.

Clamp and level combined

This dual-purpose unit is a leveller and wheelclamp in one. Such a unit is useful for touring because lack of space may mean that you don't want to take both types of device with you. It takes about five minutes to fit and then another five minutes to raise the wheel in order to level the caravan.

Lifting leveller

A handle on top of this device is lifted and wound round, thereby turning a screw that, in turn, raises a platform positioned underneath the caravan wheel. Although it is a fairly heavy item, probably weighing as much as the average wheelclamp, its action means that you can adjust the levelling height very precisely.

WHY LEVEL?

- You will probably **FEEL UNCOMFORTABLE IN BED** if your tourer isn't level – you might even roll out during the night!
- **SITTING AND WALKING** about in the caravan won't feel comfortable
- Plates, cutlery and glasses may **SLIDE OFF SURFACES**
- **AN OLDER FRIDGE WON'T FUNCTION** properly if it is at an angle. It will waste power and your food won't stay cool as the chemicals' circulation will be impaired
- **DOORS WILL SWING OPEN** – unless the travel catches are used

Chock-type leveller

This is a ramp-like device made of curved plastic. The curves mean that it fits the contours of a wheel very closely, and so may hold it in place more firmly than straight-sided devices. It also has tracks on either side for maximum grip on both the caravan wheel and the ground. Its hollow cavity can easily be filled with expanding foam to give it a little more rigidity.

Levelling blocks

Lightweight but strong, these blocks fit together like building bricks – three on the bottom, two in the middle and one on the top – to give you around 10cm of lift. Because they are easily fitted together, you can always buy a second set and use both together, for example, if you regularly pitch on slopes and need a higher lift.

Getting the caravan onto the device

Level the caravan from side to side *before* it has been levelled nose to tail and *before* the corner steadies are wound down. Read the instructions that accompany the device you are using very carefully – some require the caravan to be pushed back onto them, others require it to be pulled onto them. If you are pitching on particularly uneven ground, and will need to push the caravan onto the device, it may be worth staying hitched up and doing this before you carry on with your pitching procedure. If the device is a chock type, then the further the caravan wheel extends up the chock, from the flat end to the raised end, the greater the amount of lift. With wind-up devices, such as the lifting leveller and the clamp and leveller combined, the process is much slower and a greater degree of height accuracy can be obtained. After levelling, make sure that the caravan handbrake is on.

Making sure it's level

To ensure that the caravan is absolutely level, use a spirit level placed inside the caravan, over the axle. Only when you are satisfied that the caravan is level should you lower the corner steadies. They should just touch the ground and no more. If the pitch is on a slope, use wooden blocks under steadies to level the caravan from side to side (see page 113); if the ground is soft and the steadies are likely to sink, then a set of corner steady 'feet' can be very useful – one under each leg. These are made of tough plastic and are much larger than the floor area occupied by the steady itself, in order to spread the weight and prevent sinking. Corner steady feet usually have two holes drilled into them and curl round in a 'D' shape at the bottom. This means that wire can be looped around the 'D' and then through the foot, so that they are always attached to the legs and ready for use.

Above: With chock devices, the further the wheel extends up the chock, from its flat to raised end, then the greater the lift.

OTHER LEVELLING DEVICES

- Form **YOUR OWN VERSION OF THE RAMP-TYPE** device with a thick plank of wood and a large, square piece of wood. This can work just as well and varying thicknesses can be used to get the right levelling height

- **PLANKS OF WOOD** stacked on top of each other make an effective building-block type device for a fraction of the cost. For the best results, make sure that they are short and wide

Connecting up

With your tourer safely pitched and properly levelled, you can start to get things ready for day-to-day life. Your main task is to prepare and connect up the electricity, gas and water supplies. Once this is done you can actually begin to live in the caravan and use equipment such as the hob, water heater and fridge.

On-site security

Your first job should be to fit any security devices that you have brought along (see pages 46-49). Generally speaking, the constant comings and goings and the many pairs of watchful eyes on a caravan site make it a difficult target for thieves. But don't relax your security precautions. A hitchlock and wheelclamp are probably the two most highly visible devices and act as good deterrents. If you have an alarm fitted to your caravan, don't forget to set it before you leave the site to go on day trips. Make yourself known to your neighbours, so that they will know if a stranger is hanging around your tourer.

Water supply

Take your container over to the on-site tap marked 'drinking water'. If you have the type of container shown here, you will also have a filler pipe and handle. When it is full, screw the cap on and drop the container onto its side. Attach the handle and roll the container back to the caravan. Stand it upright next to the caravan's water inlet, push your water pump into the socket below the water filter and secure it with the clips provided. Put the other end of the pump into the container. Pull the 'cap' on the pump's pipes down so that it covers the container inlet – keeping debris and insects out.

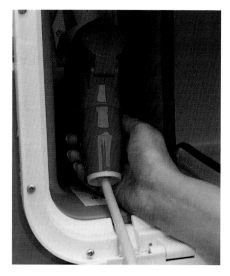

Mains electricity

Check that the main isolating switch on the RCD is switched to 'off'. Now take the mains hook-up lead and plug it into the caravan's mains inlet socket (shown here). This socket may be next to the battery as part of a built-in battery box in the side of the caravan. If the battery is inside the caravan, the socket will be in its own exterior compartment, with a flip-up cover like that over the water inlet. Uncoil the cable and take the other end over to the mains hook-up bollard and plug in.

Switch the mains isolating switch back on and check the operation of the RCD by pressing the test button (see box on opposite page). Some mains bollards have a system where the site end of the cable has to be 'twisted' after plugging in. If this is not done, the current will not flow.

WASTE WATER PIPING

Piping for waste water is sold by the metre in caravan accessory shops. It is black to distinguish it from the red and blue piping used in the hot and cold water system.

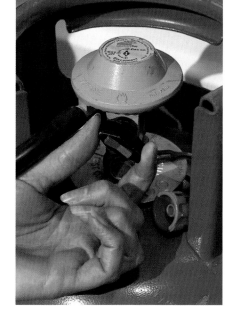

Gas supply

The first time you ever use your gas, open the gas locker at the front of your tourer, where the gas cylinders are kept, and look for a flexible orange or black hose. This hose comes from the caravan's gas system. Slip a Jubilee clip onto the end of the hose, attach the hose to the gas regulator, and then tighten the clip. Now attach the regulator to the gas cylinder. Remove the cap (if it isn't attached, keep it handy for when you get a replacement cylinder). Before fitting the regulator, check that the black sealing washer is inside the regulator itself, and in good condition. Some regulators have a nut that is tightened in order to connect them, and a handwheel that is turned to allow gas through. Others use a switch with a spring-release catch (see left). One 90° anti-clockwise turn attaches the regulator to the cylinder. When you want to use the gas, another 90° anti-clockwise turn allows the gas to flow. To turn the flow of gas off, turn 90° clockwise. If you want to unhook the regulator, press the metal catch and turn the switch 90° clockwise.

Waste water

Dirty water from the kitchen and washroom must be discarded. At the back of the caravan are one or two outlets (see top picture above). If there is just one, you will need 60-70cm of black waste piping, one end of which should go into the outlet and the other into the waste water container (bottom picture). For two outlets, use two pieces of piping about 50cm long, a 'T' piece to join them and a 20cm length that feeds from the T to the container.

Control panel

This control panel has a built-in RCD and battery condition monitor as well as the main rocker switch, making controlling, and switching between, the caravan's power sources easy. Pull-out fuses allow easy replacement and the 'pump running' light is here, too. If you run out of water, this light serves as a visual warning not to leave the pump running, a practice that can cause the motor to burn out and leave you without a water supply!

How things work

Once your gas, electricity and water are connected up, all you have to do is learn how to work your caravan's equipment properly so that you can make your stay as comfortable as possible. All the facilities are easy to use, but an understanding of how they work will ensure that you get the most from each one.

The gas system

Once the regulator is fitted and the gas turned on, go inside the caravan and locate the gas isolation taps. These are usually found under the kitchen sink area, where piping branches off to supply individual items of equipment, such as the hob, space heater and fridge. You will see a series of red knobs, one above the other. On each is a symbol that shows which equipment supply that knob isolates. If you do not turn these isolators on, the gas supply will not reach the caravan's gas-powered equipment.

Space heating

With the gas supply and relevant isolator tap turned on, begin the lighting procedure for the space heater. Turn the knob on the top of the heater round to the igniting position – indicated by what looks like a bolt of lightning. Depress the knob fully and then press the igniter button several times in quick succession. With the knob still depressed, look through the viewing area at the base of the heater to see that the burners are lit. If they are, keep the knob down for about 30 seconds and then release it and adjust the heat level. Should the heater fail to light, turn the knob back to the start and begin again.

Heating water

Your water heater will run on either gas or gas and electricity. Once you have connected your water supply, run the taps so that the heater's tank can fill up, ready for operation. If your heater is the gas-only type, it's simply a matter of switching from 'off' to 'on'. If the gas ignites and the water is heating, a green light will show. If you have a combined gas/electric water heater and want to use the gas option, the procedure is the same as for a gas-only water heater. If you want to use the mains electricity option, switch on the electricity isolation switch near the water heater controls. When the red light shows, the heater is working.

Cassette toilet

Open the door of the toilet compartment on the outside of the caravan. At the top is the tank used for flushing the toilet. To fill this for use, pull out its filler spout and pour in about 10 litres of water, plus the correct amount of fresh-smelling flushing additive. Below the flushing tank is the toilet cassette itself, or holding tank. Take this out by holding down the yellow bar and pulling (see far left). Rest it upright, pull out the spout, unscrew the cap and add toilet chemical and water. Put the spout back and replace the cassette. To empty the cassette, remove it once again. At the site's disposal point, press the yellow button that removes the vacuum, pull out the spout, unscrew the cap, and empty (near left).

Operating the lights

To operate your 12V lights, switch on the auxiliary rocker switch on the control panel. You can then switch each light on individually. These lights usually contain fluorescent tubes, which give off a lot of light while using the minimum amount of precious battery power. Lights that are powered by mains electrics will operate as long as you are plugged into the site's supply.

Making the beds up

Bedslats are wooden slats held together by webbing. Double beds are usually made up by pulling these out of a storage area and through runners found along the front edge of each seat. The front slat is usually hooked over a stopper at the end of each runner to stop the bedslats from sliding about; the last slat is fixed in the storage space. The seat cushions are then arranged on top. Bunks (bottom picture) either have to be lifted down manually from their high-level storage area and bolted into place or pulled up on a pivot system. The mattress for the bunk is often stored under a dinette.

USING YOUR WATER HEATER

IGNITING GAS-ONLY MODELS
If the **GREEN AND YELLOW LIGHTS COME ON TOGETHER**, there isn't enough power in the caravan battery to cause ignition. If the **GREEN AND RED LIGHTS APPEAR**, the heater has failed to ignite or has shut down for safety reasons – perhaps air in the gas system or no gas supply. Wait a few minutes, check that the regulator and the relevant isolator are turned on, and try again.

● **IT TAKES** about 20-40 minutes for gas-only operation to heat a tank of water; electricity-only, 40 mins-1 hour; combined gas and electricity: 20-30 mins

● The **ISOLATOR SWITCH FOR ELECTRIC OPERATION** is usually combined with the other controls or is close by, clearly labelled

Cooking

If your hob doesn't have spark ignition, hold a lighted match or igniter device close to the burner, depress that burner's knob and then turn it to full flame – the large flame symbol. The gas will light. Hold the knob down for about 10 seconds to ensure that the flame holds and to give the flame failure device (if one is fitted) a chance to warm up. The same procedure lights the grill and oven.

Adding an awning

Whether you intend to use your awning as extra living space, a sleeping area for children or guests or just as a storage area, it can prove invaluable. Many caravanners shy away from using an awning because they are thought to be difficult to erect, but follow this simple step-by-step guide and you should have no problems.

Study the instructions

1 Before you attempt to put up your awning for the first time, study the instructions carefully. Make sure all the parts are there before you begin – it will save a lot of frustration later.

Feed through the channel

2 On the side of the caravan with the awning channel (or the door side, if the caravan has channels on both sides), take the front edge of the awning and start to thread it through the wide feeder gap in the channel.

Lay out the poles

3 Once the awning has gone through all of the channel, make sure that it is centrally positioned. Now lay the poles out on the ground in roughly the same pattern that they will form when they have been fitted together in the finished frame.

GROUNDSHEETS

You will need to buy a groundsheet for your awning. On grassy pitches, these have one drawback – grass turns yellow and unhealthy if it is covered up. When booking into a site, ask about their rules. Many stipulate that you lift your groundsheet each day, or use a special type of breathable sheet, which can be quite expensive.

Put in the central poles

4 Put the central, upright pole into position and then connect it to the central bracing pole that runs under the awning roof. The centre is now up, and temporary pegging out will hold it in place.

Put in the side poles

5 Repeat this process with each side of the awning, making sure that the poles are just taut enough at this stage to hold the awning up.

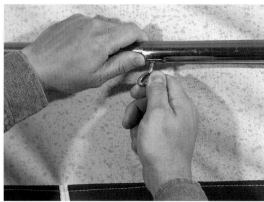

Zip up doors and windows

7 Next, go outside the awning, put in any panels and zip up the doors. This will keep the awning square while you are putting the pegs in.

Make sure it's taut

6 Slacken the bracing pole nuts and push the two halves of each pole as far apart as you can before tightening up again. These must be as taut as possible to prevent the awning from sagging or collapsing.

Put in the pegs

8 Start with the pegs adjacent to the caravan, hammering them in with a mallet. When you are satisfied that the awning is fitting correctly, hammer the rest of the pegs into the eyelets, keeping the awning canvas taut all the time.

Add the finishing touches

9 Once the awning is finished, hang the blinds or curtains supplied inside it. A correctly-erected awning will have no sags or creases, so it will stand firm in strong winds and rainwater will run off it easily, rather than collecting on top.

Caravanning with children

Because there are plenty of things for children to do on site, a caravan holiday can be a good break for parents. On a caravan park, children are out of doors, getting plenty of fresh air. They are also within the confines of a certain area, away from dangers such as busy traffic and surrounded by companions of their own age.

⚠ KEEPING CHILDREN HAPPY

- **A BORED CHILD** has the potential to ruin the holiday for everyone. Look for facilities for the right age group when you book
- Children are quite capable of **DOING ODD JOBS** around the caravan – such as fetching the water supply and helping with the washing up – and this will also keep them busy
- Encourage children to **MAKE FRIENDS** with other boys and girls on site, so that they have playmates
- Remember that **LONG JOURNEYS AND ARRIVING ON SITE LATE** at night are guaranteed to make children bad-tempered

CHILDREN'S CLUBS

More and more of the larger sites are providing children's clubs to give parents a break from childcare. These are not, however, a 'dumping ground' for children – parents are often invited to join in. Club activities usually revolve around what can be found on the park – treasure hunts are extremely popular.

Games fields

Many parks have their own games fields, where ball games of all kinds are allowed. These are situated away from the caravan pitching areas, as a stray football or cricket ball could cause a lot of damage to the easily-dented sides of a caravan. Some parks provide basketball nets and baseball hoops; and many supply mini-football nets and pitches. Games fields are often used by families for communal rounders games – a perfect way to spend a summer's evening.

Play areas

There are very few sites today that don't have at least one children's outdoor play area. These fall into two categories – traditional and adventure. Traditional play areas have the usual climbing frames, swings, slides and so on. The better-equipped adventure playgrounds have commando-style slides, rope bridges and cargo nets (see right). Wood chippings or soft impact surfaces, to cushion children in the event of a fall, are common. Some sites have indoor play areas, with pool tables and arcade games, so that children don't have to stay inside the caravan when it's raining.

Cycling and mountain biking

Caravan sites are great places for cycling, as long
as cyclists keep away from the caravans —
scratches and bumps from bicycles can cause
quite a lot of damage. The level roads that wind
around the interior of a park, plus the lack of
traffic, make sites very safe for young cyclists in
particular. Some parks with wooded perimeters
offer mountain-biking trails for adults and
children — details of these are usually found at
reception. If you don't have your own bicycle,
many parks are now offering mountain bike hire
for all the family and are happy to recommend
local off-park routes.

Indoor play

Don't forget to take along board games and
other forms of indoor entertainment. The sun
doesn't always shine on caravanners and children
get bored very quickly if they can't get out and
about. A good selection of games will keep
children entertained not only when the weather's
bad, but also on car journeys and winter
evenings, when it gets dark much earlier. Many
popular games are now available in compact
'travel' form.

BEFORE YOU CYCLE

If you or your children decide
to go cycling, run through
this five-minute safety check
before you set out:

- **BRAKES** – check the brake
tension, brake pads and
cables for damage and
inefficiency

- **HANDLEBARS, STEM,
SADDLE AND SEAT POST** –
look for damage; uneven
or loose handlebars; a
loose stem bolt; incorrect
saddle height; loose clamp

- **HEADSET** – must be tightly
fixed

- **TYRES** – must be properly
inflated, and their
sidewalls and carcass
undamaged

- **WHEELS AND SPOKES** –
Spin the wheels to check
that they run smoothly
and are straight. The
spokes must have the
right tension and be
undamaged

- **DERAILLEURS** – check by
running through the gears

- **CHAIN** – look for stiff or
damaged links

- **FINAL CHECK** – take the
bike for a quick spin, to
test the gears and brakes

- If you have **ANY
PROBLEMS**, consult a good
bike dealer (see pages
164-165)

- For some good **OFF-ROAD
ROUTES** in the UK, you
might like to consult
Haynes' *Ride Your Bike*
series

Caravan cookery

As a caravanner, you can pick your own menu and mealtimes. Make the most of this by adjusting your cooking to suit life in a tourer. For example, steam from lots of different pans forms condensation very quickly in such a compact space, so look at alternatives such as using a closed steamer or pressure cooker to prepare whole meals.

Conventional cookery

If, for example, you are cooking with a couple of saucepans and a frying pan on your hob, make sure that you have the roof-light open and, if necessary, the window slightly ajar to allow steam and cooking smells to escape. When the weather is fine, open the top half of the stable door. If you are finding steam and smells a real problem, you could have an extractor hood fitted above your cooking area. Another alternative is to fit a fan into your roof-light. This will extract air from the caravan when operating in one direction and, at the flick of a switch, bring cooling air into the caravan from outside on hot summer days.

Pressure cookery

In many ways, this is the ideal option for caravanners. The food is cooked in a sealed pan and the steam stays inside – cooking the food in about half the normal time. Soups, puddings and casseroles can all be prepared in a pressure cooker. Things can also be cooked together, so not only do you save time but you can save on gas, too. Once cooking has finished, simply open the caravan door and lift the lid outside the caravan – letting the steam out. Choose a basic model, avoiding the ones that release steam automatically – definitely not what you want in a caravan.

Caravan ovens

Although a caravan oven is much smaller than its average domestic counterpart, it is still possible to cook large casseroles and roasts – in fact, every new caravan oven comes with a roasting tray. The oven is lit in the same way as the hob and you will find that it heats up very quickly. If your caravan doesn't have a built-in oven, you could consider a small, low-wattage microwave oven. As microwaves use quite a lot of power you will probably need to be on a site that has a supply of at least 6 amps to use one – and make sure that you aren't using many other appliances at the same time.

Below: Modern caravans bring you the freedom to eat when – and what – you like, in convenient comfort.

Other equipment

All kinds of different types of cooking equipment designed for use in caravans have come and gone over the years – such as rotisseries, electric mini-ovens and portable electric rings. More recent innovations that are extremely useful in the caravan include enclosed steamers – which cook vegetables and fish using very little electricity and just a drop of water at the bottom of the unit – and multi-purpose products that can roast, poach, braise, bake or fry. Slow cookers are also proving popular in caravans because they can be left to make dinner while you're out enjoying yourself.

Right: Workspace may be tight, so choose dishes and methods that use a minimum of pans – and wash up as you go along.

Below: Your caravan oven is easily large enough to cook dishes such as substantial casseroles.

COMPACT COOKERY

- If your **KITCHEN IS NEAR THE DOOR**, watch out for children running in and out while you are cooking
- **THE HOBS IN OLDER CARAVANS** may not have flame-failure devices, so make sure that the draught from the door doesn't blow out the flame and leave the gas coming through
- Never put the **GLASS HOB-LID DOWN** while the burners are lit – the glass will shatter
- **WIPE THE WALLS** to remove cooking residue

The outdoor life

One of the best things about owning a caravan is that, even when you are simply relaxing on site, you can really enjoy the outdoor life. For example, nothing rounds off a warm summer's day better than a family barbecue, and there are now all kinds of products that make outdoor living even more appealing.

Your all-purpose awning

With all of its panel unzipped and taken out, your awning can be used as a sunshade on hot summer days. It also provides somewhere cool for pets to retreat to and is handy if there are bikes to be stowed close to the caravan, yet out of the way. If there's a sudden shower of rain, the awning makes a useful shelter, and any equipment out on the site can quickly be carried under cover until the storm has passed.

Tables and furniture

One of the most crucial items for outdoor living has to be your table and chairs set. Some forward-thinking parks provide wooden picnic benches that visitors can rearrange to suit themselves, but these are not very common. The easiest type of furniture to take caravanning is the ordinary patio table and chairs made of plastic. These are very lightweight and, if you buy folding chairs and a table with detachable legs, they needn't take up too much space and can be stowed inside the caravan when you are travelling (see pages 64-65).

Barbecues

Barbecuing is perhaps the most popular activity on caravan sites throughout the summer. However, check with reception before lighting one — some sites don't like naked fires and so will only allow the gas-fired variety that works off the caravan's own gas cylinder.

Coolboxes

Whether used for picnicking or as an extra food store, a coolbox or coolbag is a fairly essential piece of summer equipment. For day trips, you might want to buy a coolbox with a 12V lead that plugs into the car's cigar-lighter socket. This activates small cooling 'fins' inside the box, which keep food chilled. Ordinary ice-packs are a less expensive option, and many sites offer a free re-freezing service – don't forget to take them home with you!

Outdoor games

These needn't take up too much room and can provide adults and children with hours of on-site entertainment. If storage is a problem, take them along in a roof box. Boules or Petanque is a popular site game, and some parks have special surfaced areas where this game can be played. Bat and ball games with a soft and spongy ball are good for playing around caravans, and won't get you into trouble with your neighbours.

Muddy pitches

Heavy rain- or snowfalls can turn the grass on site into a mass of mud. Unless you have a towcar with four-wheel drive, the chances are that your wheels will spin and you will get stuck. If, however, you can identify exactly what you are dealing with, you can take the appropriate steps – different situations require different tactics.

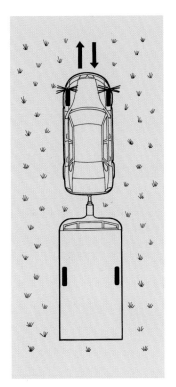

'Rocking' out

On ground that is basically firm with just a top layer of slippery mud, try 'rocking' your outfit off the pitch. Move forward very slightly by letting the clutch bite, then let the car roll back a little before engaging the clutch again to pull forwards. Put a hessian sack or some brushwood under whichever towcar wheel(s) are slipping to give them some grip.

The towrope method

If you can't pull away at all, you could try pulling the caravan off the pitch with a towrope. Unhitch and pull the car forwards until its wheels are on the site road, which will give you grip. Tie one end of the rope round the neck of the towball and the other round the hitchhead. Don't tie it to the stem of the jockey wheel, as this could cause damage. Unwind the clamp a turn or two at most so the wheel can follow you when you pull forwards – very slowly. Never 'snatch' a caravan out of mud – the towrope will break and may whiplash someone.

Deep mud

If you are stuck in deep mud, don't sit and rev the engine – the wheels will simply spin and dig in deeper. Use a spade to dig away as much mud from in front of each car and caravan wheel as you can. Hessian sacking, brushwood or even large stones packed in front of the car's drive wheels will improve the grip. Try 'rocking' as before, while fellow caravanners push the caravan. When you are free, keep your revs moderate and the steering wheel straight until you are totally clear.

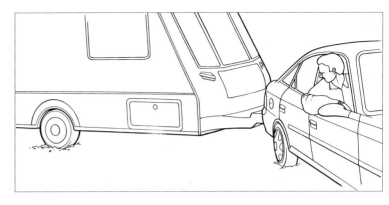

Hitching method

If rainfall has made your caravan sink slightly into the softened ground, try hitching up with the car at a 45° angle to the caravan when you want to leave. This way, when you pull off, the car doesn't have the full weight of the caravan behind it right from the start and so has the chance to get an initial grip.

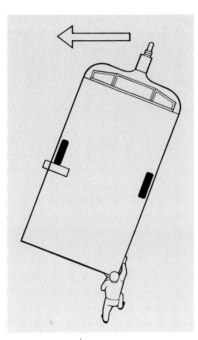

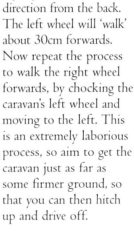

'Walking' the caravan out

If the caravan is well and truly stuck, try 'walking' it out. You will need at least one helper. Chock the back of the caravan's right wheel, take the handbrake off and pull the caravan by its drawbar as hard as you can to the right, while your helper pushes in the same direction from the back. The left wheel will 'walk' about 30cm forwards. Now repeat the process to walk the right wheel forwards, by chocking the caravan's left wheel and moving to the left. This is an extremely laborious process, so aim to get the caravan just as far as some firmer ground, so that you can then hitch up and drive off.

⚠ STAYING OUT OF TROUBLE

- Pitch **UPHILL OF THE SITE'S EXIT**, so you have gravity on your side when you want to leave
- If you want to **PITCH NEAR A RIVER**, check how spongy the banks are
- **BOOK A HARD, SURFACED PITCH**, if the site has them
- Always **USE YOUR CORNER STEADY FEET** in soft ground
- **AVOID HEAVY-HANDED STEERING** and heavy-footed acceleration in muddy conditions – you could slide into the nearest tree
- **BEFORE YOU TRY TO MOVE** the caravan, empty the gas cylinder locker. The lighter the noseweight, the easier it is to get the caravan out
- **CARRY A SPADE** and a polypropylene towrope about 10m long
- **IF ALL ELSE** fails, ask the site warden to tow you off the pitch with their tractor/four wheel drive vehicle.

Getting a grip

Snow grips or chains can be effective in mud, and not all necessitate the jacking up of the car to fit them; chocks are useful for 'walking' out a caravan. Another popular piece of equipment for helping caravanners out of mud is the gripmat, shown here. A gripmat is a brightly coloured strip of ridged plastic, sold in pairs in many accessory shops, which is very effective in giving purchase to your drive wheels. They take up very little room in the car and are an easier option than rushing around trying to find hessian sacks and brushwood.

CHAPTER 9

Caravan CARE

L ook after your caravan well and it will give you years of pleasure. A tourer is a road-going vehicle and should be treated with the same care as your car to make sure that it remains safe and in good condition. As well as taking your caravan to a professional centre for an annual service, there are lots of easy maintenance tasks and simple checks that you can do yourself. These will help prolong your caravan's life and alert you to problems while they are still in their early stages.

Keeping your caravan clean and safely maintained – outside and inside

Essential aids

There are certain items of caravan-care equipment that you should always try to keep together. They will help you in those small emergencies where a problem could have been sorted out straightaway – if only you'd had the right equipment to hand. They'll prove indispensable if there's a minor accident or if a small running repair is needed.

First aid box

Keep all of your first aid equipment – plasters, bandages, scissors, dressings, safety pins and so on – together in one box that has been designated as the first aid box. Make sure everyone who uses the caravan knows where it is.

Screwdrivers and adjustable spanner

Don't take your entire toolkit with you! An adjustable spanner and a couple of screwdrivers – a mix of flat and cross-heads – will take care of most tasks.

Warning triangle

If you are unfortunate enough to break down, place the triangle 30m (100m on a motorway) behind the caravan to warn other road users. Carrying a triangle is compulsory in some countries. Make sure you buy an approved one, which will have the code ECE 2703 on it.

Moist hand wipes

Buy a large box of wipes – you'll almost certainly use it. Towbar grease on your hands, quick clean-ups after running repairs and various other mishaps are quickly sorted out with a couple of these.

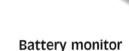

Battery monitor

Hook this up to your caravan battery and it will tell you how much power you have left. The type shown is quite expensive, but less sophisticated ones are available at a lower price. A monitor, or a battery charger with LCD to indicate its condition, is especially handy if you're charging your battery at home while you're not using the caravan.

Pliers, insulating tape and sharp knife

You'll be glad you've got these if your cables drag on the ground and wear through. Without road lights on the caravan your holiday could be over. Cut out the damaged section, strip back the insulation, twist the wires together and insulate them with the tape. This will keep you on the road until you get a repair.

All-purpose oil and spray lubricant

Squeaky corner steadies, stiff locks, stuck hinges, stubborn catches... if your oil can't get at these, then spray lubricant will. A pipe that fits onto the nozzle helps you reach the most difficult places. Also useful for the small on-site jobs that always need doing to your car – or to a bike you've taken along.

Tyre health

Your tourer must have a set of healthy tyres in order to be able to take to the road safely, yet, as with all too many cars, the tyres on a caravan tend to be neglected. Damaged and incorrectly inflated tyres are a major cause of traffic accidents, so do everything you can to make sure that yours are fit for the road.

Left:
Cracks in your tyres mean that it's time to replace them.

Tyre health check

Check your caravan tyres regularly – before every trip out at the very least – and leave enough time before you travel to buy replacements if necessary. The most vital checks are those on the actual fabric of the tyre, including the sidewalls; don't think that all you have to do is check that the depth of tread meets the legal requirement and that the pressure is acceptable. Remember that a tyre has two sides – make the effort to look at the inner side as well as the easily accessible outside.

Cracks and bulges

The appearance of cracks and bulges mean that your tyre has been damaged and must be replaced. Some damage, such as shallow cuts, can be repaired, but the safest course of action is to buy a new tyre. Cracks are usually caused by UV light and ozone, especially if the caravan sits in the road or driveway between trips, with its wheels still on (see pages 142-143). Bulging and abrasions are often the result of impact, such as hitting a kerb when cornering too tightly, so always check your tyres very carefully if this happens while you are towing.

Under- or over-inflation

Running on under-inflated tyres causes the outside edges of the tread to wear more quickly than the inside, gives poor handling and increases fuel consumption. Over-inflation wears out the centre of the tread and reduces road-grip. Most insurers will refuse to pay out on car/caravan accidents if any of the tyres are not at the manufacturer's recommended pressures.

Tyre types

Try to fit the same type of tyres (for example, radials) to the van as those on the car. Tubeless tyres must only be fitted to wheels with safety rims. If in doubt, consult a specialist tyre dealer.

SPARE WHEEL CARRIER

If you don't have the room or facility to carry your spare wheel inside the caravan, you could buy and fit a spare wheel carrier. This one (right) has been made by a chassis manufacturer to fit underneath most caravan chassis, without any need for drilling or complicated fitting. The spare wheel is then bolted onto the cradle. Don't overlook your carrier and tyre when you are carrying out maintenance checks, and keep moving parts well-greased and free of grime and road salt.

CHANGING A WHEEL

Warn others

1 When you get a flat tyre, pull over and try to get off the road. If you can't, warn other drivers by putting your warning triangle out on the road and switching on your hazard flashers. Leave the car and caravan coupled and put the caravan handbrake on. Lower the jockey wheel to take some of the weight off the tyres.

Prepare to jack up the tyre

2 Put chocks behind the wheel opposite to the one you are changing. Now *start* to undo the wheel bolts with your caravan brace – loosening them just enough to take away the tightness – *before* attempting to jack up the wheel. If you try to unfasten the bolts while the wheel is jacked up and off the ground, the wheel will spin and you will find the task extremely difficult. (Note that the brace supplied with new caravans is seldom adequate.)

Position the jack

3 If the caravan has its own jacking point (consult your handbook), place the jack there. If not, then place it under the caravan's axle, as close to the chassis as possible. Use a jack that is designed for caravan use – an ordinary car jack is not suitable for a caravan's axle.

Change the wheel

4 Jack the caravan up to allow just enough room for the wheel to be removed. Now provide extra support by lowering the steadies on the same side as the jacked wheel. You should never, however, use the steadies to raise the caravan – this will damage them. Remove the bolts, put them aside and replace the wheel.

Lower the new wheel

5 With the old wheel laid flat, safely out of the way, put the bolts back – 'finger-tight' only at this stage – and start to lower the new wheel to the ground. Once it is firmly on the road you can use your wheel brace to tighten the bolts without the nuisance of any wheel-spin.

Tighten the bolts correctly

6 Tighten the bolts in the following sequence: North, South, East, West (or 12 o'clock, 6 o'clock, 3 o'clock and 9 o'clock). Now raise the steadies, stow away your tools and the old wheel, raise the jockey wheel and take off the caravan handbrake. Don't forget your warning triangle and the chocks! Proceed straight to a garage to have the bolts tightened to the caravan maker's recommended figure with a torque wrench.

Battery maintenance

Your caravan's 12V battery – running the low-voltage electricity system – is a lifeline when you are caravanning. If you've left your mains lead at home or run out of gas you will still be able to work the water pump, power some lights and use 12V appliances. A caravan battery is completely different to a car battery, and so its care is different, too.

Right: With caravans that have an integral battery compartment, access is via a lockable door on the exterior.

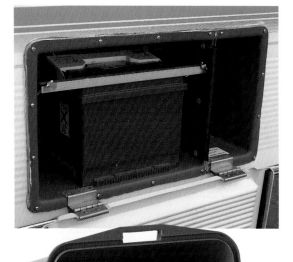

Right: For caravans without built-in battery compartments, a special box can be fitted inside the caravan to house the battery.

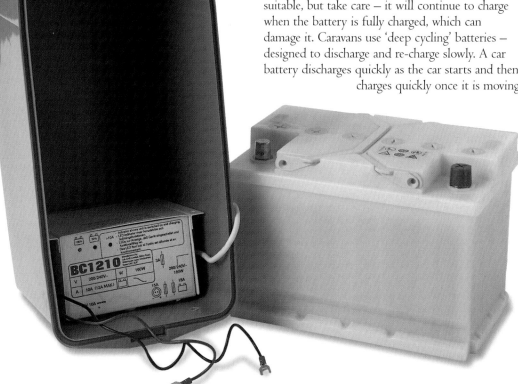

Inside or out?

Most caravans have an integral compartment on the outside of the caravan that houses the 12V battery. With caravans that don't have this compartment, a battery box can be fitted inside – usually under one of the front dinettes or at the bottom of a wardrobe. There are two main stipulations for this sort of battery. First, air must be able to circulate freely around the box while charging is underway, and it must be vented, above the battery, to the outside of the caravan (see *Battery charging*, below). Secondly, the box must be acid-resistant, as a charging battery gives off hydrogen fumes – which are lighter than air.

Battery charging

As well as being able to charge the caravan battery from the car while you are on the move, you can also use a special caravan battery charger to charge it at home. A car battery charger may sometimes be suitable, but take care – it will continue to charge when the battery is fully charged, which can damage it. Caravans use 'deep cycling' batteries – designed to discharge and re-charge slowly. A car battery discharges quickly as the car starts and then charges quickly once it is moving.

SAFETY NOTES

- Don't forget to **CHECK THE CONNECTORS** in your battery box regularly (it is the connectors that you hook the battery up to in order to detect signs of wear and tear)

- If you are **CHARGING WHILE DRIVING WITHOUT THE TOURER** in tow, never let the connectors touch each other, or the car body (this creates sparks)

- Always **USE THE STRAPS OR METAL BRACKET** in built-in battery compartments to secure the battery in place while you are on the move

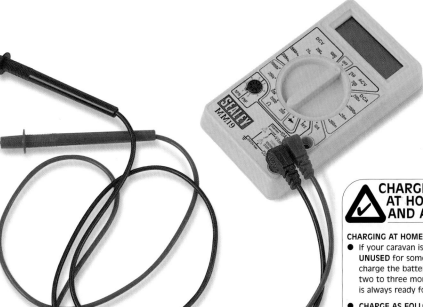

Right: A device like this can be used to monitor the condition of the battery when it is not in the caravan.

Checking battery condition

A device called a multimeter or voltmeter – available from your caravan accessory shop – will tell you what condition your battery is in when it is not in the caravan. (When it *is* in the caravan, you can tell the battery condition by looking at the control panel, which either has a condition indicator or two lights, which show respectively whether the battery is alright, or needs charging.) A voltmeter takes its reading from the terminals. If a battery has been discharged completely and left that way for 24 hours or more, a re-charge followed by a condition check is vital. If the reading does not register 12.5+V (indicating a full charge) then the battery has probably been damaged beyond repair. A reading of 12.4V shows a battery that is 50 per cent discharged; 10.6V or less indicates a fully discharged battery.

Looking after your battery

From time to time, take your battery out and give it a thorough health check. Observe the usual removal precautions – the connection(s) to the car should be unplugged and all appliances should be switched off in the caravan. Then, take a good look at the casing. Are there any cracks? If there is grease and grime at the top of the battery, wipe it off. Clean the terminals with soft glass-paper until they appear metallic again and smear a blob of petroleum jelly on each to protect them. If your battery is the top-up type, check the electrolyte levels and fill as needed with distilled water (from your car accessory shop).

ABOUT BATTERIES

Caravan batteries – also called 'leisure batteries' – are bought from caravan accessory shops and are specially designed to charge and re-charge slowly. Modern caravan batteries have six connected cells, housed in polypropylene casing, and each cell has a set of positive, and a set of negative, plates.

There are two kinds of caravan battery – the sealed, maintenance-free battery and the 'top-up' variety. If yours is the latter kind, remove the vent plugs or strips and shine a torch into each cell to check the electrolyte level. Top up with distilled, de-ionized water if the plates are exposed.

The caravan battery is rated in Ampere hours. The current is delivered at a specified rate – for example, a 60Ah battery, at a 20-hour rate, gives the stated 60A capacity if the battery is discharged over 20 hours.

⚠ CHARGING AT HOME AND AWAY

CHARGING AT HOME

● If your caravan is **LYING UNUSED** for some time, charge the battery every two to three months so it is always ready for touring

● **CHARGE AS FOLLOWS:** Switch everything off in the unhitched caravan, uncouple the negative (earth) terminal first and then remove the battery to a cool place

● **OBSERVE THESE RULES:** Keep the battery out of children's reach; don't place on a concrete floor, or it could discharge itself; choose a well-ventilated area where there is no danger of any sparks; never smoke – a charging battery gives off inflammable hydrogen gas

● When you put the battery **BACK INTO THE CARAVAN**, always connect the negative (earth) last

CHARGING ON THE MOVE

● **MAKE SURE THE BATTERY** is well-ventilated and not near the source of a spark. Strap it into position, preferably in a battery box like the one on page 136

● If you are **ON SITE FOR SOME TIME**, you can charge the caravan battery in the car boot while you're driving around without the caravan in tow

● If you want to **CHARGE WHILE TOWING** (and already have the correct wiring, with relays, to do this), locate the cable that corresponds to the pin for battery charging. Using battery terminal connectors, connect into it (for the positive supply to the battery) and link the negative feed to a suitable earth point on the car

Cleaning your caravan

Your tourer will probably lie unused for reasonable stretches of time, so you will need to give it regular spring-cleans. Maintaining a clean and tidy caravan will not only make it much more pleasant to use, but will also increase its potential resale value and keep appliances and equipment functioning efficiently.

Wipe the hob

1 Cleaning your hob regularly will help to keep it working properly and safely. Use a cloth and spray cleaner to clean the hob itself and the burner tops. Take off the tops and wipe inside with a damp cloth. This clears any residue left by saucepans boiling over, which can easily block the gas jets.

Keep your fridge fresh

2 Like any fridge, a caravan fridge becomes stale-smelling when switched off for a while. Use a suitable fridge cleaner to remove food remains. Racks and shelves are easily removed and can be washed in warm, soapy water — or bicarbonate of soda and water if you want no trace of a soapy smell.

Clean your soft furnishings

3 If your curtains are cotton, then you can wash them at home; curtains made of imitation velvet must be dry-cleaned. If you are not sure whether your curtains are washable, patch-test a small area with lukewarm water and a mild detergent. Follow the same rules for upholstery and cushion covers.

Care for the carpet

4 Try to keep any carpet clean — this is the soft furnishing that takes most of the knocks. Because of the limited space, it's tempting to walk right inside before taking off muddy boots, but try to resist. A mini vacuum cleaner that re-charges off the mains is always a useful tool to take with you.

Cleaning upholstery

5 If you have tested your upholstery (see Step 3) and found that it's washable, you could try steam-cleaning it. This is especially convenient if the covers are not removable. Use a small household steam cleaner or a steam wallpaper remover to raise dirt to the surface. Brush it off when the upholstery is dry.

Look after sinks and drains

6 Your kitchen sink will be enamelled or stainless steel and can be cleaned with a spray cleaner. The wash-basin, mouldings and shower tray in the washroom are acrylic, so wash them with warm, soapy water after every use to avoid damage and scratches. To neutralize smells, put a spoonful of bicarbonate of soda down each plug-hole or outlet and flush through with hot water.

Clean the windows

7 As caravan windows are acrylic, they should be cleaned with extreme care, using a very soft cloth, clean water and a chamois leather. Otherwise, you will begin to see small scratches all over them. You can try removing all but the deepest scratches with a brass-cleaning or jeweller's polish, as shown here. Put a dab of polish on a lint-free cloth and work into the scratch in circular motions to effectively 'polish' out the scratch.

Keep drawers and lockers tidy

8 Always empty and clean out drawers and lockers after every trip, or you may attract insects and vermin. You can line lockers and drawers with thick wallpaper to protect surfaces, as shown. Then simply throw the wallpaper away if necessary after your trip.

EXTERIOR CLEANING

Keeping the exterior of your caravan clean – with a proprietary cleaning product – will stop the development of ugly black streaks, running down from the corners of the trim. If left, they will simply grow darker and more unsightly. The caravan roof should be cleaned too, as green mould can flourish here. Use a soft, long-handled brush to get at the high places. Hard bristles may damage paintwork and washing with a high-pressure jet may strip the paint from the aluminium skin. A pair of stepladders is essential.

Preparing for storage

Many caravanners take their caravans off the road and store them away for a part of the year when they won't be touring. If you want to store your tourer, there are certain essential points you should know in order to choose a safe and secure site, and various things that you should do before you put your caravan in mothballs.

⚠ HOW CAN I BEAT THE THIEVES?

- **FIT ALL OF THE SECURITY DEVICES** you can (see pages 46-49), even if you are convinced that your caravan is in the safest possible storage site. Choose really heavy-duty devices if you can. Storage sites are generally quiet places, and a determined thief will have plenty of time to work away at freeing a caravan

- **TAKE OFF THE WHEELS.** A wheel-less caravan is very unattractive to a thief

- **TAKE OUT ALL OF YOUR BELONGINGS** and open the curtains, so that a potential thief can see that the caravan is empty

- **KEEP A PHOTO** and a good description of any distinguishing or security marks at home, just in case it is stolen. These will be invaluable to the police

Emptying the water system

This stops water stagnating in the system. It also stops freezing and damage to pipes, leading to more problems when a thaw comes. Open the taps in the caravan and drain away any water. Now locate the casing for the water heater vent and remove the drain plug to ensure that all of the water in the system is drained off (you could also have a 'drain down' tap fitted into the supply system). Another, very easy, option is simply to fill the system with 'potable' anti-freeze prior to laying the van up and flush the system through prior to its next use. To ensure that the system is clean before you leave the caravan, flush it out with a sterilizing solution (see page 87).

Soft furnishings

If possible, take seat cushions and scatter cushions out of the caravan and store them in a warm, dry place in your house. If you don't have enough space at home, simply stand all cushions up on end in the caravan. They may need to be propped up against each other, but should touch as few hard surfaces as possible. This way air can circulate around them and stop them from becoming damp.

In the washroom

If your cassette toilet has an upper chamber (which holds the water and chemical for flushing), now is the time to empty it out completely. If you don't, the water may freeze in extreme weather conditions, cracking the chamber as it expands. If you aren't planning to have the caravan off the road for too long and don't want the bother of emptying and refilling the chamber, just add a little anti-freeze liquid, as you would in your car's water bottles.

Battery care

Keep your caravan battery charged and ready for the new season – otherwise you may be starting your touring year off with having to buy a new one. Charge the battery in situ – if you have access to the caravan and it has battery-charging facilities on board and you are also near a mains supply – or take the battery out and charge it at home with a suitable charger (see pages 136-137).

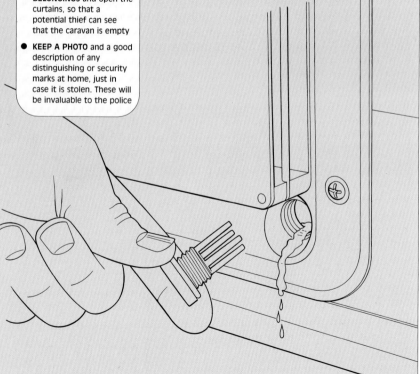

Left: Find the water heater vent, on the outside of your caravan, and remove the drain plug to drain off all the water in the system.

Tyres and wheels

If you are putting your caravan into storage, the best thing to do with the wheels is to take them off. If tyres are left with the weight of the caravan on them they will gradually deform and become 'square' – which will ruin them. UV also affects tyres, so store them away from sunlight, in a garage, for example. When removing your tyres, jack the caravan up, put it in axle stands and place a cover over the bare wheel hubs to protect them from water ingress of any kind. Better still, jack up the caravan, remove the wheels and fit axle stands or a protective, lockable 'winter wheel' to each hub – this will also act as a deterrent to thieves. If you do have to leave the tyres on during storage, rotate them frequently to stop deformation and protect them with a special anti-UV cover (available from accessory shops).

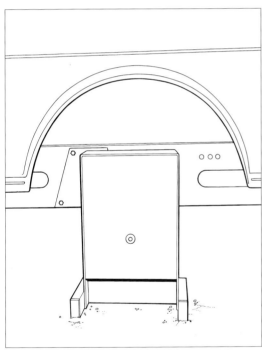

Above: Winter wheels not only protect your tyres but are also an excellent security device as they are locked into place and make the caravan impossible to tow.

A good clean

Make sure that your caravan is thoroughly clean inside and out before stowing it away (see pages 138-139). A good exterior waxing with car polish will keep out weather, dust and dirt. Using a hose pipe, wash down the chassis underneath the caravan to get rid of any salt and road dirt.

Preventing fridge mould

Mould is likely to develop if you leave the fridge switched off for a while with the door closed. Once you have cleaned your fridge thoroughly (see pages 138-139), leave the door on the wider of the two door catch settings (see pages 156-157). This lets just enough air into the fridge to stop it from going stale and mouldy during storage.

Protective measures

If you don't plan to fit a heavy-duty hitchlock while the caravan is in storage, then put some form of cover on your hitchhead. Think also about setting your caravan alarm system (see pages 152–153). With the steadies down, take the caravan handbrake off before you take your leave – this will ensure that it doesn't seize up in the 'on' position while the caravan is lying dormant.

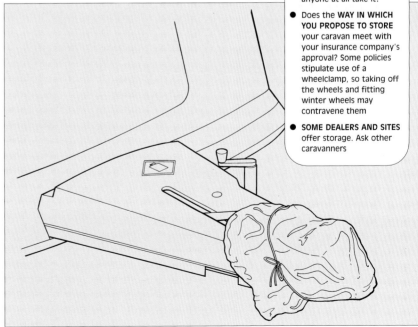

Right: You can get special hitchhead covers from caravan accessory shops or improvise with a plastic bag, as shown here. Whatever type of cover you choose, make sure you secure it so that no water or dirt can get in but air can still circulate, to avoid condensation.

SECURE STORAGE

Some storage advice has already been given on page 48, but here's a complete round-up of the points you should consider

STORAGE AT HOME
- **THERE'S NO REASON** why you can't store at home if local rules allow it and you have the room, as long as you take security precautions. Note that taking off the wheels to render it immobile means you'll need a dedicated space for the caravan
- Storing at home means that you will be able to **KEEP A CLOSER EYE** on your caravan, checking inside occasionally

CHOOSING A STORAGE SITE
- **IS THE SITE FULLY ALARMED** or has it got 24-hour security patrols?
- **CAN YOU ACCESS** the caravan whenever you want to check it over?
- Is the caravan **BEING STORED NEXT TO** anything that may damage its chassis or running gear? (For example, fertilizer on a farm storage site)
- Do you need **PROOF OF IDENTITY** to get the caravan out, or could anyone at all take it?
- Does the **WAY IN WHICH YOU PROPOSE TO STORE** your caravan meet with your insurance company's approval? Some policies stipulate use of a wheelclamp, so taking off the wheels and fitting winter wheels may contravene them
- **SOME DEALERS AND SITES** offer storage. Ask other caravanners

Cold climates

As caravans are generally well-insulated and heated, caravanning in wintry conditions and using your tourer as a base for winter sports are perfectly possible. Some caravans are better-equipped for the cold than others – look for the word 'winterized' and for some mention of on-board plumbing and water tanks in the manufacturers' literature.

WINTER SITES

Look for sites whose literature states that they are open all year round. These sites will be equipped for taking visitors in the worst of winter weather. Their toilet blocks will be heated and they will ensure that however low the temperature is, there will always be a supply of drinking water. Sites close to ski resorts often have boot stores, equipment lockers, drying rooms and even common rooms, for get-togethers on long, winter evenings.

Keep it clear

If you intend to go caravanning where snow will be falling, don't let your caravan get snowed in – always take a shovel with you. You should patrol around the caravan every day, especially after heavy snowfalls, and dig out any snow that has drifted under the caravan. This way, you will ensure that air can circulate under the caravan and keep the gas drop out holes (see page 21) from getting blocked from below. You will need to fit special covers to your fridge vents (available from caravan accessory shops) to prevent it from over-freezing.

USING GAS IN WINTER

If you normally use Butane gas, switch to Propane for winter caravanning. Butane freezes below 0 °C, whereas Propane stays liquid right down to -40 °C.

In order to use Propane, you will need either a Propane regulator or a Propane changeover unit. The latter fits Propane and Butane cylinders simultaneously and so is handy for changing between the different types of gas.

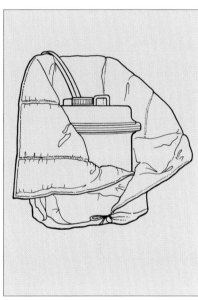

Cover up

Anything kept outside on the ground needs to be shielded, either from heavy snowfalls or from the problems of sitting on muddy grass – which can freeze solid and make whatever is sitting on it stick fast. The generator shown here has been encased in a special cover made of tough nylon, and mains cables and water containers must also be covered. Put specially-designed plastic feet or blocks of wood under your corner steadies. Any items that are outside should be moved slightly every day to stop them from being buried in frozen ground or solid ice.

Insulate well

Special insulating covers like this are ideal for external water containers – to keep them cool in summer and prevent freezing in winter. Emptying your waste water container each night stops backflow if the water freezes and you fail to notice. Some tourers have an on-board water tank, ensuring that the water supply stays liquid, or you can simply store your container inside overnight. The best way to protect water pipes is to buy a caravan with internal piping or to have this added. If this isn't possible and your tourer has pipes running underneath the floor, then lag them thoroughly.

CHAPTER 10

Caravan
KNOW-HOW

Once you have owned your caravan for a while you may well want to personalize it a little, adding or changing certain things in order to make your touring life more comfortable. You may also want to understand a little more about how some of your tourer's equipment works, and look into ways in which you can improve its efficiency. This chapter provides you with all of this, plus two handy reference features – a glossary of caravanning terms and an A-Z listing of invaluable contacts.

TV aerials, interior decoration and beating condensation are just some of the subjects covered

Caravan makeover

You may feel that your caravan is in need of a facelift. Most people are unlikely to try anything as skilled as replacing the furniture, but you'll find that there are all kinds of subtle changes that will make all the difference. Watch your weight and space – don't be tempted to replace caravan fittings with more substantial domestic ones.

Right: Replacing light fittings is an easy way to bring the look of your interior up to date.

Left: If you make your own shower curtain, you'll be able to have exactly the size you want.

Lighting

If the light fittings are looking rather old-fashioned, remove them. Measure right around the top and the base with a dressmaker's tape and then look for something lightweight that's a little more up to date, or that suits a new colour scheme you are working to.

Carpets

The easiest way to give your floor covering a new look with minimum fuss is to buy a long, hallway-type rug. One of these will usually cover most of the caravan carpet between the seats and up through the kitchen/washroom area. Because they are usually quite thin, they will not add a lot of bulk to the existing carpets. A whole carpet can be replaced, but caravan carpets are often held in place by being laid before the furniture is screwed down. This means that completely replacing your carpet involves unscrewing and lifting the front edges of all the furniture.

Washroom

One of the main ways in which you can improve the shower area is by adding a new curtain (if washroom curtains are left in situ during periods of storage, black mould often forms along the bottom edge). If you need to renew your shower curtain you may want to make a new one yourself – a domestic one might be the wrong size and weight. Again, measure the drop and width of the curtain and save the fastenings from the old curtain to sew onto the new one. If you felt that your old curtain was a little narrow, here is your opportunity to add a few extra centimetres.

Left: Give cupboards a facelift by adding stylish new handles.

Left: Make sure that any new covers have zips in them, so that they can be cleaned easily.

Furniture

With the right equipment and materials, it is fairly straightforward to replace locker lids and internal doors. Or, you could simply give doors and lockers a facelift by fitting new handles. Remove one of the original handles and, as well as taking it around caravan accessory shops to find a replacement with the same distance between fixing points, try DIY stores for something in a totally different style.

Soft furnishings

You can have a specialist company make a new set of covers for your upholstery, by fitting the fabric to the original foam, or ask them for totally new cushions. But this can prove expensive. A cheaper option is to buy purpose-made loose covers that simply zip over your existing cushions – they will probably have to be of stretchy material to ensure a fit – or to make your own. If your original upholstery was not removable, try to add zips so that you can remove covers for cleaning. If the foam in your cushions is getting old, you may find it has deteriorated and is uncomfortable. New foam can be bought and cut to fit, but it must be fire retardant; you can also buy fire retardant spray for your soft furnishings. (Look in caravanning magazines for upholstery products and companies.)

Curtains

If you change your upholstery, you will probably want to change your curtains to match. Plain material is best, as even small patterns can look too fussy in the confined space of a caravan. If your current curtains are a little skimpy, put some extra

Left: As with the shower curtain, don't discard the fixings from your old curtains when replacing them, as domestic curtain fixings are often too large for caravans.

BUYING FABRIC

Make sure that you buy the right sort of fabric for upholstering. Look for one that is washable (either machine or dry-clean) and crease-, dirt- and fade-resistant. Ask the retailer to recommend something hard-wearing that won't show stains and marks readily. If you want a pattern, choose a small print that won't be overpowering in such a small space or lead to waste when you cut pieces up in a way that will make the pattern match properly. Choose a plain, cotton-type fabric for the cushion-cover lining.

material into the new ones and line them to keep out the sun in the mornings and provide some additional insulation for caravanning out of season. Unpick the tape and remove the hooks from the old curtains and transfer it to the new ones – domestic size tape and curtain hooks may be too large for the fixings.

Central heating

If you have been caravanning for a while, in all weather conditions, you will really appreciate the comfort of having a space heater. If you intend to tour out of season, take part in winter sports or holiday in colder climates, you should look at either changing to a caravan with a type of central heating system, or having one fitted.

Below: This blown-air outlet is in a caravan washroom. The central disc can be opened to let the warm air through when the blown-air facility is in operation.

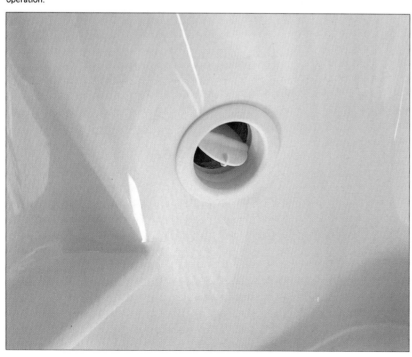

How do caravan heaters work?

The two main types of caravan heater are the flued and catalytic varieties. The flued kind is by far the most popular, drawing its combustion air from outside the caravan rather than from the living space, via a special inlet. It is also the safest, and can be left burning 24 hours a day if necessary. The principle behind the flued heater is its aluminium heat exchanger. Although the heater does contain a naked flame, this is in an enclosed chamber and allows complete combustion of the Liquefied Petroleum Gas (LPG) from the caravan's own supply before it meets the exchanger. The heat of the products of combustion are transferred into the caravan as they travel up and along the top of the heater and then down through other chambers. The thermal drive created by the rising column of hot gases from the flame keeps the combustion products moving around in this way. Once all of the heat potential has been extracted, the combustion products leave the van by a sealed flue at the bottom of the heat exchanger.

In contrast, a catalytic heater is designed to burn only a small amount of LPG on start-up. Gas and oxygen are then combined to form a mixture that releases heat when passed over a catalyst. This process produces a certain amount of the potentially hazardous gas, carbon monoxide, so good ventilation is essential. Catalytic heaters are uncommon today.

Blown-air heating

An easy way to upgrade from an ordinary caravan heater to a central heating system is to have a blown-air enabling kit fitted by your caravan service centre. This kit allows the distribution of warm air generated by the heater, via a fan, to different areas of the caravan – usually the front and rear ends, plus the washroom. In addition, these fans can usually be used independently to circulate air around the caravan when the heater is not in use, to provide some relief on hot summer days. Introducing a blown-air kit consists of adding the fan to the back of your existing heater, putting in ducting for the warm air to pass down and adding small vents for the air to pass through into the chosen areas of your caravan.

Fan boosters

One relatively recent introduction is a more powerful type of warm-air fan booster – operated by a wall-mounted control panel – that is able to create heat from either gas or mains electricity.

The control panel has a thermostat that is used when the booster is running on mains electricity; when it is running on gas, the temperature is controlled by the thermostat inside the gas heater (when the heater is on it

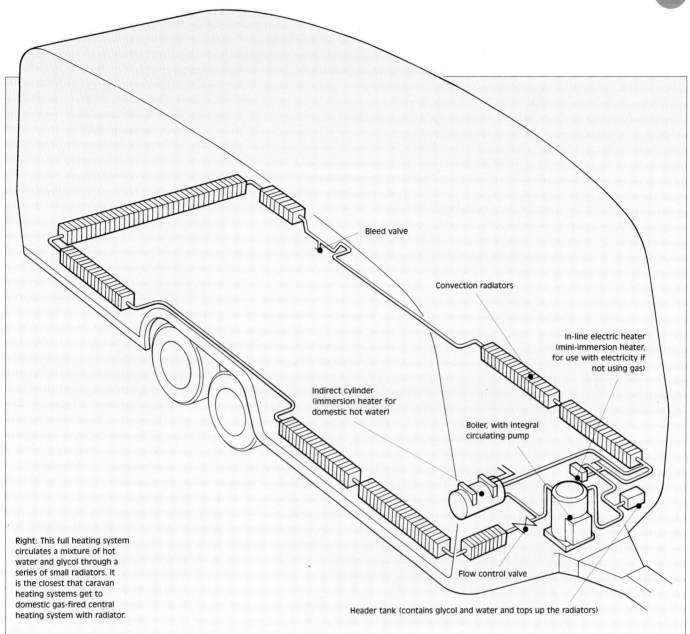

Bleed valve

Convection radiators

In-line electric heater
(mini-immersion heater,
for use with electricity if
not using gas)

Indirect cylinder
(immersion heater for
domestic hot water)

Boiler, with integral
circulating pump

Right: This full heating system
circulates a mixture of hot
water and glycol through a
series of small radiators. It
is the closest that caravan
heating systems get to
domestic gas-fired central
heating system with radiator.

Flow control valve

Header tank (contains glycol and water and tops up the radiators)

simply distributes the warmth it is producing).
The booster runs quickly when the heater is at a
high temperature, so that it can circulate warm
air around the caravan rapidly. When the
temperature approaches the level set on the
heater thermostat, gas input to the heater slows
down. The fan also slows down, to avoid
producing cool draughts.

The heater thermostat on the control panel
also has a setting to circulate air around the
caravan without heat, for summer use, and to
draw heat from its integral 2kW electric element
and circulate that. When the temperature set on
the control panel thermostat is reached, the
electrical input is reduced to 1kW and the fan
speed drops.

'Wet' heating systems

So-called 'wet' heating systems – developed in
Scandinavia – are very popular and are perhaps
the best type of system for colder climates. These
work basically by heating up a mixture of water
and glycol and passing it around the caravan to
small 'radiators' that run all around the inside of
the caravan's walls. The heat from the radiators
rises up from under the seats and furniture and
into the body of the caravan, much like a domestic
central heating system does.

Temperature is regulated by a thermostat and
there may even be a facility to heat water. Systems
like this can turn a small caravan washroom into a
handy mobile drying room for wet clothes, but
leave a window open to prevent condensation.

 **HEATER
TIPS**

- **NEVER TRY TO REPAIR** a
caravan heater yourself –
leave it to experts

- **HAVING A BLOWN-AIR KIT**
with a 12V fan fitted is far
cheaper than having a
system with a 2kW mains
fan fitted

- One advantage of the
NEW MAINS FAN TYPE is
that the site's electricity –
for which you are paying a
one-off fee – is being
used, and not your leisure
battery

Beating condensation

Condensation can turn into a real problem, especially when touring in colder weather, when it's warm inside but chilly outside. Older caravans often suffer particularly badly. Although condensation may seem at times like an insoluble problem, there are effective steps that you can take to minimize it.

What causes condensation?

Condensation – the moisture that is produced when warm air from breathing, cooking and so on condenses on cool surfaces such as walls and windows – is caused by inadequate insulation and a lack of ventilation. Older, timber-framed caravans tend to have wall insulation made from glass fibre.

Below: Modern acrylic windows have much the same effect as domestic double-glazing.

This insulation is usually packed between gaps in the framing and is prone to dropping down towards the bottom of panels, leaving cold spots further up the walls. Glass fibre is still used in some caravan roof cavities where the roof shape makes it difficult to use the usual roof insulator – expanded polystyrene.

The sandwich bonding techniques used by most caravan-makers today use expanded polystyrene (white) or Styrofoam (blue) insulation as a 'filling'. The average thickness of this insulation is 22-25mm in the caravan walls, with thicker sheets in the floor. Thick sheets are used in both the floor and walls of caravans that are designed for regular use in cold climates.

Improving insulation

Little needs to be done to improve insulation in new caravans, but older caravans may benefit from covering the interior walls with a special wall covering, made from PVC or vinyl foam, which can help to keep them warmer and so reduce condensation. The best treatment for lack of insulation in older caravans is to strip out and replace the old glass fibre insulation, but this is a major undertaking, not worth attempting which, for health reasons, should only be done by professionals.

Improving the insulation of the floor can be done by buying flame-retardant, 25mm foam sheeting from a DIY outlet, cutting it to shape and fixing it to the underside of the caravan with a strong adhesive. Provide additional support for any large sheets of foam by screwing wooden battens into place.

Use your ventilation

The law dictates that caravans must have a specified minimum area of fixed ventilation that should never be obstructed – especially in winter when the windows and door are shut. Additional

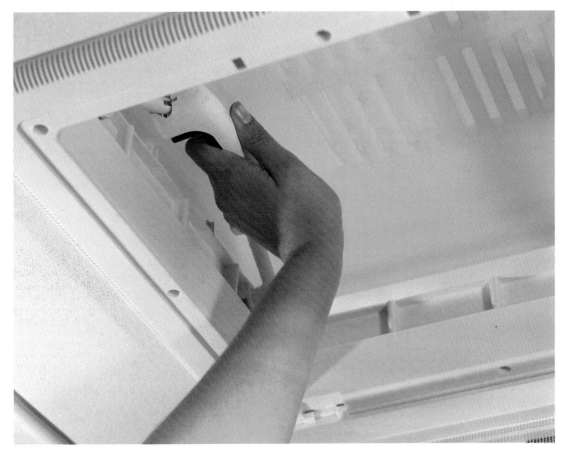

Left: Condensation appears when domestic tasks – space-heating, running hot water, cooking and so on – are carried out in the confined space of the caravan. Make sure ventilation is used wherever possible – the roof-vents are there for a good reason.

MAKING SLATTED TOPS FOR BEDS

Making a slat system is a relatively easy DIY job. Measure the width between the seats and buy smoothly planed softwood battens about 30mm x 12mm deep. Buy enough battens to allow a space of 8cm between each one and enough upholsterer's webbing to put two strips the full length of the slats down each side. Space out the slats and tack the webbing to the bottom of each one. Remember to put a stopper on the ends of each side of the seats, to stop the slats moving during the night.

ventilation, such as the caravan's roof-lights, should be used to cut down condensation from domestic tasks. It is also possible to have extractor fans fitted over the hob area to transport steam and smells outside the caravan. Such devices are relatively cheap and don't take long to fit.

Other measures

If you are on site and find that you need to give your window insulation a temporary boost, try taping cling film, strong plastic or polystyrene sheeting (if you don't mind not being able to see out!) over the inside of the windows. Another option is to buy made-to-measure 'Silver Screens', which also keep out summer heat. Fitting thermal blinds or adding a thick or thermal lining to curtains will help to keep things warmer at night.

If you have solid plywood bedbox tops instead of slats, and condensation gathers under your seat cushions, you can alleviate this problem by drilling holes into the plywood. Also, try placing a thick blanket under the seat at night, to soak up some of the condensation, airing it off during

the day. If you have to use the caravan's tables to make up the bed, this will add to your condensation problems. It's a simple DIY job to make and fit removable slats as your bed base, and these allow air to circulate. You could also make slats for the top of bedboxes – fix them at the back of the seat top but always make sure that you fit a device such as a small bolt at the front so that you can roll them back easily for underbed access (see box, above right).

Windows

All but the cheapest modern caravans are fitted with double-skinned acrylic windows, giving the same effect as domestic double glazing. Older caravans have single-pane glass windows. These can be updated by replacing them with the new acrylic versions. Contact the manufacturer of your caravan to find out about availability. If these units are not available, you can always fit perspex or acrylic insulating sheeting on the inside of the windows. Look in your local DIY outlet for UV-stabilized acrylic sheet that can be cut to size and fixed into place with rubber draught insulation strips screwed to the wall. This sheet can then be removed in summer.

How alarms work

A good alarm system is always an excellent investment. It will usually have one or more features that detect an intruder moving around inside the caravan, and/or movement of the caravan itself. Knowing more about what the various features do will help you to choose a system that will provide the best protection.

Infra-red sensor

A Passive Infra-Red detector (PIR) is a sensor, about the size of a fist, that is positioned inside the caravan. It detects any heat sources (such as intruders) moving around in the caravan. PIR units are better at detecting objects moving across their field of view, rather than towards them, so bear this in mind when you are positioning the unit. Nearly all surfaces radiate a certain amount of heat, and things such as sunlight coming through a window or a space heater that has been left on could trigger your alarm. If a pet that keeps low to the ground, such as a dog, is to be left inside your caravan, it may be a wise investment to buy a special lens for the unit that only detects movement in the top third of the caravan's interior.

Pressure mat

A pressure-sensitive mat is another option. This can either be left just inside the door, under the doormat, or (in case the thief anticipates this and steps over it to gain access) somewhere in the main body of the caravan, under the carpet. Pressure mats are a good alternative to PIR sensors, where false alarms are likely.

Door contacts

These have magnetic contacts and are fixed – one on each side – to a moving and non-moving part of a door – that is, the door itself and its frame. As soon as the door opens, the contact is broken and the siren goes off. If you were to use door contacts, PIR sensors and pressure mats, you would have a pretty thorough all-round interior security system.

Tilt sensor

For detecting movement of the caravan itself, a tilt sensor is needed. This gives a signal if the caravan tips slightly forwards or backwards (if the jockey wheel is raised and the caravan is being hitched up, for example) or from side to side (while the caravan is being towed away, for example). It is inactive when the caravan is level. Most tilt sensors can be adjusted so that they will only react to substantial movement (such as hitching up) and not to gentle movement such as rocking by the wind. However, if the sensor is not set properly this can lead to false alarms. A sensor that detects nose-to-tail movement is less prone to the effects of strong winds than one that senses side-to-side movements.

Corner steady sensor

In addition to corner steady locks (see pages 48-49), there are also corner steady sensors, which are generally mounted directly onto a steady. These detect the winding action of the brace on the steady nut. In a 'quick-stop' situation, such as at a motorway service station, where you are

unlikely to want to put the steadies down, there are also detectors that bring the car's electrical connections into the alarm circuit. Any changes in the voltage of the circuit, such as the thief driving off with the connections coupled and then braking, or opening the door and allowing the courtesy light to come on with the caravan coupled up, will trigger the alarm siren.

Some recommendations

Try to fit an alarm that has its own batteries or, if it has to run off the caravan's own 12V battery, make sure that there is an anti-tamper circuit (so that the thief cannot cut the wires and disarm the alarm) or a back-up power source. The same is true if the battery can be accessed from the outside (for example, by levering open the battery box). If you want to leave your pet dog in the caravan while keeping your alarm on, use door contacts on the main door and any other openings. Corner steady sensors fitted to two or more legs are also useful in this situation. If you fit a tilt sensor, make sure that you don't desensitize it too much – or it may not react to a thief hitching up very carefully.

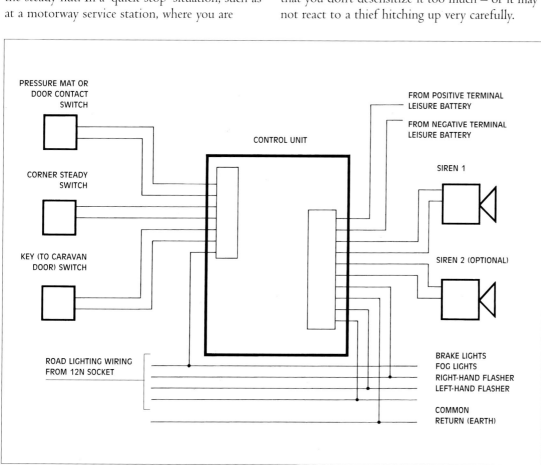

Left: This diagram illustrates how the infra-red alarm shown on page 48 would be wired in the average caravan. Most alarms are easy to fit and use, requiring little or no technical knowledge.

⚠ POINTS TO CONSIDER

- If the alarm is **POWERED BY THE CARAVAN BATTERY**, make sure that there is an anti-tamper circuit/standy-by power source in case the thief disconnects the battery or cuts wires

- **CORNER STEADY SENSORS** and door contacts are ideal for pet owners

- **ALARMS DON'T TAKE LONG TO FIT** – somewhere between 1½ and 4 hours. You can fit them yourself, or have them fitted professionally, at your local service centre

- If possible, **CHOOSE A KEYPAD** rather than a key to operate the alarm – keypads are simple to use, and keys are easy to lose

- Some companies offering **CARAVAN INSURANCE** will give discounts if you have alarms fitted. Insurers often specify which kinds of alarms make you eligible for a discount, so it's always worth a phone call if you are thinking about which one to get fitted

- When it comes to **POWER CONSUMPTION**, remember that systems running off the caravan's battery do place a drain on it. PIRs with a flashing red light to warn intruders of their presence use more power still. If you want to lay your caravan up for a period of time with the alarm activated, it's worth checking the condition of the battery every so often to ensure that it isn't being drained

- If you don't want to drain your leisure battery, or you want to remove it for charging while the caravan is in storage, you might want to consider **AN ALARM SYSTEM WITH ITS OWN POWER SOURCE** – again, check the batteries regularly

Manoeuvring with ease

Not everyone storing their caravan at home between trips has a wide, totally flat drive – and the more difficult the caravan is to manoeuvre out onto the road, the more reluctant its owners will be to use it to the full. Movers and winches will help you to get the most from your tourer and there are aids for hitching-up, too.

Right: Most winches are designed to pull caravans up slopes (as shown here), not to lower them down. For this job, buy a purpose-designed braked winch and follow all the instructions carefully.

CHOOSING AND USING A WINCH

You must choose a winch with the right puling factor. To work this out, do the following simple sum – then double the result to be on the safe side. Multiply the weight of your caravan by the gradient of the slope you need to pull it up. For example, a 900kg caravan and a 1 in 5 slope (20%) gives this: 900 x 1 ÷ 5 = 180.
So you will need a winch with a pull of 180kg.

If you don't know the gradient of a slope (say, your drive), work it out by using a clothes line to measure first its length, from top to bottom, and then its 'rise'. To measure the rise, get a helper to stand at the bottom of the drive, holding a broomhandle, and run the line horizontally from the top of the drive to the handle. Then divide the rise by the first length to get the gradient. For example: a 2.5m rise ÷ 10m travel = 25%, or 1 in 4.

Caravan winch

These units have a cable that is attached to the caravan and is used to 'haul in' rather than 'lower' it. They run on one of three power sources: domestic mains electricity, 12V and manual operation (winding by hand). The winch unit is either attached to any strong, fixed structure that can be found nearby or to a mobile point (the towcar). The end of the cable is then hooked to the caravan, either to the hitchhead or the chassis.

Each winch manufacturer recommends the best place for this; some even provide kits to make the job easier.

Depending on its design, a winch will have a stated pulling factor. This factor is just a fraction of the caravan's weight, as most of the caravan's mass is being transferred to the ground. See the box on this page for details on working out this factor so that you can choose the correct winch.

Left: A motorized jockey wheel can allow just one person to manoeuvre large, heavy caravans – especially moving them up gentle slopes.

Motorized movers

These relatively expensive pieces of equipment are designed with an integral shaft that replaces the jockey wheel in the jockey wheel clamp. They are powered by the caravan's own battery, via a set of leads that clamp on to it. This may mean moving the battery temporarily into the gas locker while manoeuvres take place. (NB: because of the spark risk, do not use crocodile clips on the battery terminals if you still have a gas cylinder in the locker.) Some manufacturers supply long extension leads, so that the battery can be left in its box while the mover is in use.

There are usually 'on', 'off', 'forward' and 'reverse' switches on the mover's handle, which is also used to steer. A gentle walking pace speed makes control easy, although the strain on the battery is quite severe on start-up, so the device should always be connected to a fully-charged battery. One solution to this problem is to keep another, fully charged caravan battery at home, solely for use with the device. Traction can be poor on grass or gravel – you might need a helper to sit on the A-frame so that you get extra grip!

Hitching-up aids

If you have to hitch up on your own for some reason (see pages 90-91), then a hitching aid could prove useful. These can be simple – say, a shaped shield that is bolted between the faceplate and towball and 'guides' the hitchhead over the ball; or more complex – for example, a cable that fixes to the towball and is attached at the other end to a winding mechanism next to the hitchhead. This is then 'reeled' in until the head is over the towball.

Replacement jockey wheels

A manual alternative to the motorized movers are manually-driven ratchet jockey wheels. These fix to the caravan in a similar way to their motorized counterparts. They are only really suitable for fit people to use – to create movement via the ratchet means either pumping or turning the handle, which can be quite an exhausting process.

> ### ⚠ DO YOU NEED AN AID?
>
> - **WHEN BUYING A CARAVAN**, think about the length and slope of your drive and work out if you will need an aid. If you have to reverse up your drive, will it be too steep for you to do so without continuous stalling? When you get to the top, is there room to turn the outfit around to unhitch the car? Do you lack the confidence or skill to manoeuvre a caravan up a steep, narrow driveway?
>
> - If you are **BUYING A LARGE CARAVAN**, will help always be at hand to manoeuvre your tourer? If not, an aid will give you total independence
>
> - **ONCE YOU DECIDE TO BUY AN AID**, weigh up which will suit your needs. If you are using an aid that cannot be used to lower a caravan down a steep slope, consider how you will do this. For example, is there enough room at the top of the drive to allow the caravan to be swung around so that the car can be backed up and hitched, ready to drive the caravan down?

Fridge efficiency

A caravan fridge is a crucial piece of touring equipment. Because it can run on 12V, mains electricity and gas, you may find its operation rather confusing when you first start to use it. Once you have mastered this, there are various things you can do to get the best performance from your fridge, in both summer and winter.

How fridges work

The application of heat – from any of the three power sources – causes a coolant to circulate though a system of pipes and fins to keep the fridge contents cool. When using gas, the products of combustion pass through a sealed flue that releases them on the outside of the caravan – not to be confused with the fridge vents on the side of the caravan.

Running the fridge on 12V

The 12V operating option is only possible when the towcar's engine is running, via the electrical connections (see pages 74-75). If it were to run permanantly off the caravan's 12V source or off the car battery while the car engine was turned off, it would soon drain either of these. The main reason that the fridge can be run on 12V is to keep food cool while you are on the move and not running on one of the other power sources – mains electricity from a site or the caravan's gas supply. The fridge should be filled and then pre-cooled on either mains electricity or gas, before being switched over to 12V for the journey.

Operating on gas or mains electricity

The gas option should only be used while the caravan is stationary – either on site or while the caravan is standing in the driveway, being loaded. It is dangerous to tow your tourer with the fridge operating on gas – naked flames are not allowed at petrol stations and most motorway service areas. Remember to turn on the gas isolator tap, or the gas supply will not be able to reach the appliance.

Left: Between trips, make sure that you leave the fridge empty and clean, and the door slightly ajar. Leave the door on the special catch at the top (on the inner of the two main holes). This means that air can circulate freely in the fridge whilst it is not in use and lessen the chances of mould forming.

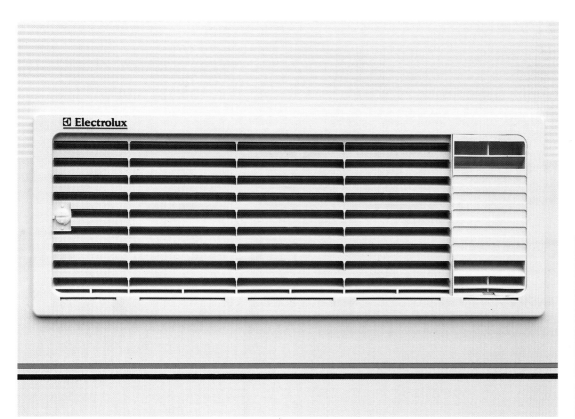

⚠ FRIDGE CARE

- Have your fridge **SERVICED PROFESSIONALLY** every year, at the same time as your caravan has its annual service

- **DURING FERRY CROSSINGS**, when the car engine is off, the 12V fridge operation will also be off. Your fridge contents should remain cool for short crossings, but if your sea journey takes longer than about three hours, it is best to buy food on arrival

- **TO PREVENT SPILLS** and smells, always store liquids in containers with tight tops, and wrap up cheese and other strong-smelling foods very thoroughly

- On the road, **USE THE TRAVEL CATCH** on the setting furthest from the fridge body. This will keep the door shut tight so that the fridge can't disgorge its contents en route

- In most caravans, you will **NOT BE ABLE TO EXTINGUISH THE GAS FLAME** by turning the control knob to its lowest setting. The only way to switch off the gas is to turn it off at the fridge gas 'cock' (usually in a cupboard) or at the gas cylinder

Once you have successfully ignited the fridge, the temperature control dial can be turned to the required setting. Check that the fridge is lit by looking through the viewing window (usually in the bottom left-hand corner of the fridge) for a small blue flame. As long as you have the correct regulator, caravan fridges can be run off either butane or propane gas.

Perhaps the simplest way to run your fridge – if you have the facility – is off mains electricity. Once you've connected your caravan to the site's supply, set the rocker switch on the fridge at the 'plug' symbol and then select the temperature.

Getting optimum performance

A caravan fridge requires two other things to operate safely and efficiently – its vents mustn't be blocked, and it must be level.

When it comes to vents, don't forget to check for less obvious obstructions that may not block the vents totally, but will impair their performance. For example, your caravan door may cause a partial blockage when it is open, or a small porch awning might cover the area just around the door where the vents are. If you are caravanning in winter and find that the vents let in a draught, then the fridge hasn't

been correctly installed. The fridge should be re-installed, with correct shielding around the rear cooling unit. Never try to block vents with paper or cloth as you will interfere with the cooling process of the fridge.

Older fridges must be level to operate properly, so put a spirit level on the freezer compartment shelf when you're levelling your tourer. Modern fridges usually work perfectly efficiently on uneven ground. If in doubt, check with the fridge manufacturer.

Coping with hot climates

If you will be caravanning in hot weather, don't over-pack your fridge. Leave space around things so that the cool air can circulate and do its job. Cool food beforehand in your domestic fridge and then run the fridge on gas or mains electricity for up to four hours before you set out, so that the contents will keep as cool as possible while you are on 12V. If you are on a crowded site, where there are so many tourers drawing from a hook-up that there's a power loss, your fridge may not be able to cool food efficiently and you should change over to gas. Caravanners who are travelling around can always switch back to electricity on reaching somewhere where the voltage is higher.

All about gas

There is much more to using gas than simply turning it on and lighting it. It is important that you know how to choose the best type of gas for your caravanning needs, are able to use it in the safest possible way, and understand the value of maintenance. On a site without mains electricity hook-ups, your gas supply could be your lifeline.

Gas types

Liquefied Petroleum Gas (LPG) is refined crude oil, and the most commonly used varieties for caravanning are propane and butane. At normal temperatures and pressures LPG is gas, becoming liquefied when more pressure is applied. Because a small volume of liquid is equivalent to a large amount of gas, even a small cylinder of LPG will last a long time. Once the gas is in use, the temperature at which it changes from being a liquid to a gas (ready to be used by the caravanner) is crucial – butane is useful for warmer conditions, while propane is better suited to colder climates (see *Gas System* page 21). Butane gives a greater heat output than propane, but propane can run more appliances and is better suited to those caravan appliances that demand a lot of gas.

How much gas do you need to take?

Some caravans make this choice for you – there may only be two storage spaces for medium-sized containers in the gas cylinder locker. Also, if storage is in a front locker you'll be restricted by your noseweight. On average, a medium-sized (6-7kg) cylinder will last about five days; a small (4.5kg) cylinder about three days. Some caravanners keep a large propane cylinder outside their caravan, but this is not particularly safe. Because a big cylinder probably won't fit in the gas locker, you will be transporting a large amount of gas, unsecured, in the car boot and then leaving an unsecured cylinder outside the caravan, where it might fall over or be tampered with.

Gas safety

Always put safety first when dealing with LPG. It is highly flammable when mixed with air, so leaks are a potential hazard. As LPG is odourless, it contains a 'gassy-smelling' agent to make leak-detection easier. Leaks are likely to occur in the flexible hose that joins the copper pipework of the caravan's gas system to the gas regulator. If you see any signs of damage on this hose, get it replaced by a qualified gas fitter or your caravan service centre.

Regulators themselves sometimes fail, so buy a replacement if you are in any doubt. Never turn on the gas and try to test for a leak in the gas system – leave it to a qualified gas engineer.

Left: To connect the regulator to the gas cylinder so that you can use your gas supply, you have to access it through the gas locker. The principle is the same for changing the regulator from an empty bottle to a full one. Some caravans have an access flap inside the caravan, on the front windowsill, allowing you to reach into the locker and change the regulator from the comfort of the caravan.

⚠ ✓ USING YOUR GAS SUPPLY

- **BUYING GAS:** With some companies, you sign a hire agreement for the cylinder. With others, you buy the cylinder outright. Whichever system is in place, you buy the gas the cylinder contains. When a cylinder is empty you simply exchange it for a full one, paying only for the gas.

- **RESPECT YOUR GAS** supply. If you suspect a leak, turn the gas off at the cylinder and seek professional help

- **SELECT THE type** of LPG you will use with care

- If you are **TOURING IN A DIFFERENT COUNTRY** and have to use the same type of gas but in a different-sized cylinder, you may find that your regulator will not fit. Make sure you take the correct one with you – check the details with a club or motoring organization

Regulators and changeover valves

The regulator does just that – it regulates the flow of gas from the cylinder to the appliances in the caravan. The two gases require different regulators – as the internal pressure of each type is so different – and the fitting of each is also different. Butane regulators have either a push-on connection with a small washer inside, and a dial with 'release', 'locked' and 'gas on' positions. Other butane cylinders, such as those sold by Camping Gaz and available worldwide, have a screw-in regulator that contains a leak-proof valve. Check that the black sealing washer is in place. Turn the regulator control to the 'closed' position and screw the regulator onto the cylinder. It is normal for the safety device to make a noise when the regulator is shaken. Propane regulators are screwed into place and have a stopcock for turning the gas on and off.

Whichever type of gas you are using, it's possible to connect up two cylinders and swap from one to the other when the first becomes empty – without having to disconnect and reconnect the regulator – by using a 'changeover valve'. Changing cylinders on a cold, wet night isn't enjoyable, so this can be a good investment. If you use the automatic version that's available, make sure you keep an eye on the gauge that shows when the first cylinder is empty and get a new one immediately – or you could find yourself with two empty cylinders late on a winter's night.

Improving TV reception

If you want to take a TV with you, you should ideally choose one that requires only a moderate amount of power at start-up and when running, and so can use the on-site electricity supply. The alternative is a TV that runs off your caravan battery – best suited to tourers with on-board charging facilities, if you're a regular viewer, so that the battery isn't drained.

Types of aerial

To receive television signals in your caravan you will need an aerial, just like at home. There are four main types of caravan aerial available.

1. The external directional aerial

This is similar to an ordinary household aerial and, if correctly positioned, is the best kind for capturing a signal. It will have either 7, 9 or 12 elements (crossed strips) – 7 is suitable for strong-signal areas; 9 for normal-signal areas; 12 for places where the signal is poor. The aerial must be attached to the caravan at a point high enough to clear nearby obstructions, such as other caravans or trees. Look

around the site and see which way other people's aerials are pointing, then copy this yourself.

2. External omni-directional aerial

Many modern tourers come with these already fitted – although you can easily fit them yourself. They look either like flying saucers (with a case covering the elements) or have an open lattice of exposed elements, and receive every available signal from all directions, so there is no need for adjustment. They are supplied with signal boosters, which maximize sound and picture quality or can also reduce the signal if you are too near to a transmitter.

3. Indoor directional aerial

If you seldom watch TV, an inexpensive aerial that plugs into the set and sits on top of it or nearby will probably serve your needs. The best type is one with its own battery-operated signal booster.

4. Built-in loop

This comes with the TV and is usually permanently fixed to the back of it. Because the loop is in a fixed position, which may not be the best one for receiving a good signal, this type of aerial tends to be easily affected by outside interference.

Satellite TV

It is perfectly possible to enjoy satellite TV while caravanning. Satellites are strung out in different orbital positions, so, before investing in any expensive equipment, find out which area is covered by the channels you are interested in – a channel that you receive at home may not be available where you will be touring. The signal from each satellite falls on a certain area of the Earth – this is known as its footprint. The closer you are to the centre of the footprint, the stronger the signal will be. Finding out about this will tell you the minimum size of dish required. A small dish (45cm) may be sufficient at the centre of the footprint, whereas a 120cm

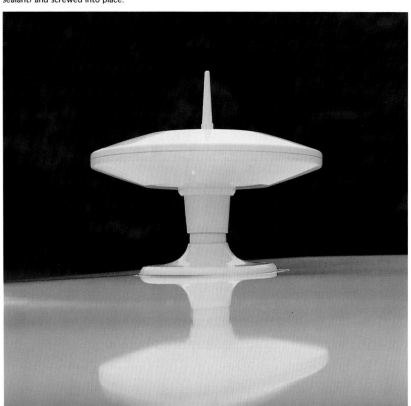

Below: Fitting a TV aerial, such as this omni-directional version, is easy. The best place to drill the hole that feeds the co-axial cable into the caravan is over the wardrobe area. The wires can then be run down the inside of the wardrobe and out to where the TV will sit – usually on a table next to the wardrobe. The base of the aerial is fitted over the hole (coated with sealant) and screwed into place.

Left: Most modern caravans are fitted with an aerial socket like this, and many are also fitted with an external omni-directional aerial, either at the factory or at a dealer's service centre.

version may be necessary towards the outside – but will this be practical to carry around and store when not in use?

The combined power consumption of a TV and satellite system means that you will have to use mains electricity. A satellite beam cannot penetrate obstacles; even thick cloud-cover or a tree can interfere with reception, so pitch where nothing will block the signal.

Watching TV all over the world

Unless you have a multi-standard set, your TV may not be able to pick up transmissions in other countries, as systems differ from one place to another. Most of Western Europe uses PAL B/G, except for France, Luxembourg and Monaco, which use SECAM L. A few other countries, including the UK and Ireland, use the PAL I system. Eastern European countries are on SECAM D/K, as are some African countries. Most of North Africa and parts of the Middle East use SECAM B/G.

Getting a good picture

If you are a long way from the local transmitter or situated in a depression, you will get a 'snowy' picture. Conversely, if you are very close to the local transmitter, the signal might be too strong and you may get a 'herringbone' pattern on screen. In either case you can either strengthen or weaken the signal by using a variable signal booster/reducer.

On-screen ghosting is caused by an external obstruction, so fix the aerial as high as you can to clear this, or move to another pitch. You may also find that you get interference caused by electrical equipment such as fans, fluorescent lights, electric shavers and so on. Turn these off while watching the TV, or wire the TV directly to the 12V power supply (the battery) rather than into another 12V supply cable, which may be carrying interference. You can also buy suppressors for fitting into offending fluorescent lights.

The best television set

If you will be using mains electricity, there are quite a few TVs that you can take along. If you want a TV that operates on a 12V supply, the choice narrows. Black and white TVs use far less power than colour ones. To work well, some sets need at least 12V of power, so on-board charging facilities (now pretty common) are necessary. A long length of cable between the battery and TV causes a voltage drop, so remember this when selecting your 12V TV.

Video recorders

It is quite difficult to find 12V VCRs and, although some mains units are available that are suitable for caravanning use, these usually offer a playback facility only (not record). If you do have a compatible VCR with record facility and you want to take it abroad, make sure that the appropriate PAL or SECAM transmission works there, or you won't record anything at all.

⚠ ✓ **AERIAL FIXING TIPS**

● **ONCE YOU HAVE THE RIGHT LOCATION** for your aerial, drill a hole for the co-axial cable before fixing the base into position

● It is important to use **PLENTY OF SEALANT** (from your caravan accessory shop) around the aerial base so that water cannot get in

● Keep the **WIRING TO THE AERIAL POSITION** neat, using cable tidies to clip it to the inside of the wardrobe

● **USE AS SHORT** a length of co-axial cable as possible between the aerial and the TV – the picture quality will then be better

● **FOLLOW THE AERIAL MAKER'S INSTRUCTIONS** carefully when doing the wiring

● **IF YOU HAVE RECEPTION PROBLEMS** once you have fitted the aerial, call the makers

● **WHEN WORKING ON THE CARAVAN ROOF**, don't kneel or rest on it – it will not support your weight. Get a helper to hold the ladder steady and to be on hand to assist you

Glossary of terms

A

A-frame The part of the axle that projects out at the front of the caravan's body and houses the hitchhead, jockey wheel, handbrake, the electrical connections between the caravan and car and the breakaway cable.

Awning A canopy or tent-like structure attached to the side of the caravan to add extra living space. One edge is fitted into the caravan's awning channel; the rest is then supported on poles and pegged out.

Axle A part of the chassis. Basically a steel tube with the caravan's wheels at either end.

B

Bedslats A system of wooden slats held together by webbing. They are pulled out of a storage area and across the gap between seats, to form bed-bases.

Berths The number of beds in a caravan. Also a way of gauging the size of the caravan – a two-berth caravan cannot be used by more than two people, for example.

Breakaway cable A cable designed to pull on the caravan's brakes and bring it to a halt if the coupling between the car and caravan fails.

Butane A type of Liquefied Petroleum Gas (LPG) used by caravanners. Suited to touring in temperatures above 0 °C only.

C

Cassette blinds Silvered blinds that are housed in a tidy casing and used in caravans instead of/as well as curtains. Flyscreens – to keep out small insects while the windows are open – usually come with the blinds, in the same casings.

Cassette toilet A caravan toilet that is permanently sited in the washroom and collects waste in a cassette underneath. The cassette is accessed for emptying via a door on the outside of the caravan.

Central heating A system of caravan heating that is roughly the same as the central heating at home, except that lightweight pipes are usually used rather than domestic-style radiators. Some caravans come with this already fitted, especially those designed for use in very cold climates.

Corner steadies The 'legs' found at each 'corner' of the caravan, used to stabilize the caravan when it is pitched and you are living in it.

Corner steady winder A winding device used to raise and lower the corner steadies.

Coupling The 'link' between car and caravan. On the caravan side, this is the hitchhead; on the car side, the towball. The hitchhead fits over the towball and locks around it. Electrical connections from the caravan plug into special sockets at the back of the car, next to the towball, to allow the caravan's road lights to mimic those of the car.

D

Drawbar see *A-frame*.

E

Electricity This comes as either a low-voltage supply (12V, from the caravan's own battery) or a high-voltage supply (mains electricity, from a special plugging-in point on site). All caravans have some equipment that works off the 12V supply, and many now have a mains facility and equipment that works off this source. Mains electricity is charged at a flat fee by the site.

Ex-works weight What the caravan weighed when it left the factory – that is, unladen. Also known as the Unladen Weight and Design Weight.

F

Flame-failure device A device found on many caravan gas appliances, which switches off the gas supply if a lit flame blows out.

Flyscreens see *Cassette blinds*.

Folding caravan A type of caravan designed to fold down into a compact shape that is lower, and only slightly wider, than a car. This makes it easier to store and tow than a conventional rigid-sided tourer. It can be erected in minutes.

G

Gas see *Butane* and *Propane*.

Gas drop-out holes Small, round holes in the caravan floor – usually under beds or in cupboards – that allow any escaped gas to 'drop' through (because it's heavier than air) and leave the caravan instead of building up inside it. The holes are usually covered with wire mesh to keep insects out, but should never be obstructed.

Generator This produces electricity for use in the caravan. Generators are usually petrol-driven, making busy sites quite noisy. If you're on a rural site without mains hook-ups and you don't have battery-charging facilities, a generator could be useful.

Gross weight The weight of the caravan when it is fully loaded. This must not exceed the Maximum Design Weight (the maximum amount of weight that the caravan has been designed to carry), which is also known as the Maximum Laden Weight.

H

Hard standing A pitch on which the usual grass has been replaced by gravel, concrete or another hard surface. They are especially useful in winter, when the ground gets soft and towing the caravan off can be difficult.

Hitchhead The device at the very front of the caravan with a small handle on top that is used to connect the caravan to the towball. Also called a coupling head.

Hitching up The act of linking the car and caravan together.

Hitchlock A security device that fits over the hitchhead to prevent someone else hitching up to your caravan and towing it away.

J

Jack The device used for lifting your caravan when you want to change a wheel. The best types are the side jacks built integrally with the chassis. There is also an airbag type that caravanners find useful, and this inflates from the car's exhaust via a special pipe. This type spreads the weight of the lifted caravan and does not put a strain on one particular area under the caravan's chassis.

Jockey wheel The small wheel at the front of the caravan that holds up the A-frame (and therefore the nose of the caravan) while it is not hitched to the car. It is wound up and clamped safely out of the way while the caravan is being towed.

K

Kerbweight The weight of a car without a driver or passengers, but with a full tank of fuel plus everything that comes with the car as standard (spare wheel, toolkit and so on). You need to know this figure in order to calculate which caravans your car can tow safely. Your local car dealership should be able to tell you the kerbweight of your particular model and year of car.

L

Leg winder or **brace** see Corner steady winder.

Leisure battery The kind of battery specially designed for

caravan use because it loses its charge slowly. A leisure battery can be repeatedly discharged and re-charged without damage to the 'plates' inside. It powers the caravan's 12V functions and equipment.

Loading Margin The amount of weight that you are allowed to add to the caravan when you are loading. The Loading Margin is the difference between the Unladen Weight and the Maximum Design Weight. These three figures are supplied by the caravan manufacturer, and must be adhered to.

LPG Liquefied Petroleum Gas – the type of gas that is used in caravans.

M

Mains Mains electricity.

Mains cable (hook-up cable) A cable that connects with the on-site mains hook-up at one end and the caravan at the other, to bring mains electricity into your tourer.

Mains hook-up The on-site socket where you plug into the mains supply.

Matching (or Outfit Matching) The act of choosing the right caravan for your car, or vice versa.

Maximum Design Weight or **Maximum Laden Weight.** This figure is the maximum weight that a caravan has been designed to carry, and should never be exceeded. Caravan manufacturers often call it the MDW or MLW.

N

Noseweight The maximum downward-bearing load allowable on the towball when the car and caravan are hitched up (that is, stationary). Usually given by the car manufacturer.

Noseweight gauge A device used to measure noseweight.

Number plate It is essential that you carry a number plate on the back of your caravan that matches the one on your car.

O

Overhang The distance between the rear axle of a car and the point where the caravan meets the car (that is, the towball). On a car with a long overhang, the caravan may rock from end to end using the towball as a pivot point – very uncomfortable for rear seat passengers. Shorter overhangs create far more stable outfits.

Over-run brakes Caravan brakes, so-called because they act when the caravan tries to over-run (that is, run into) the towcar. When the caravan pushes up against the car as it brakes, the caravan's brakes are applied.

P

Pitch The area where you put your car and caravan while you are on site.

Pitching The act of siting your caravan on a pitch. Also the name given to the nose-to-tail rocking seen in some caravans while they are being towed.

Pop-top caravan A compact caravan with a central roof area that the owner raises and locks into place on site, creating a normal amount of headroom.

Portable toilet The alternative to a fitted cassette-type toilet, suitable for those whose washrooms aren't large enough to install the latter type. The portable model is a compact unit that either sits in the washroom or, if there's no washroom, in the main body of the caravan (usually stored in the wardrobe during the day and only brought out at night). The one drawback is that the cassette has to be carried through the caravan for emptying.

Propane Another form of LPG, which can be used all year round, as it will still become a gas at temperatures down to -40 °C.

R

RCD Residual Current Device and Residual Current Circuit-Breaker (previously known as an ELCB – Earth Leakage Circuit Breaker). A switch turns itself off if there is a sudden change in the supply of mains electricity in a caravan – to stop possible electrocution.

Regulator A device that fits on top of a gas cylinder to regulate the flow of gas into the caravan's gas system.

Running gear The name given to all of the components that allow the caravan to be towed on the road – the chassis, brakes, axle and wheels.

S

Sandwich construction The method used to build caravan walls and floors, which 'sandwiches' insulation between sheet material (plywood and aluminium).

Snaking When the caravan takes on a pendulum effect that gradually swings the car out of control.

Space heater The name for any caravan heater that warms the 'space' inside a tourer, as opposed to heating up the water.

Stabilizer A device to 'stabilize' the car and caravan and stop unwanted side-to-side or up-and-down movements while towing.

T

Through vision When a caravan's front and rear windows are large enough – and not obstructed by any furniture or fittings inside – the driver can look right through the tourer, via his or her rear-view car mirrors, to keep an eye

on any traffic behind.

Torque The turning power of a car's engine, which determines whether or not it will be a good towing vehicle. Torque that peaks at a low rpm is good for caravanning.

Towball The 'hook' at the back of the car that goes under the hitchhead to join the caravan to the car. The towball is fixed to, or is part of, the towbar.

Towbar (or tow bracket) The fixing underneath the car to which the towball and electrical connections are attached.

U

Undersealing A layer of water- and weatherproof coating underneath the caravan.

Unladen Weight The weight of the caravan as it leaves the factory, with all its fittings but no load.

W

Washroom The name for the caravan's bathroom.

Waste water container The container, usually black or grey, that is sited under the caravan to collect used water from the kitchen and washroom.

Wheelclamp A security device that clamps around the wheel on the caravan and prevents the caravan from being moved.

Winter wheel A large, angular device that fits in place of a wheel using the normal stud or wheel bolt fixings while the caravan is being stored. This not only keeps out dirt and allows the tyres to be stored away from harmful UV light, but because it is locked into place and renders the caravan untowable, it can also act as a security device.

A-Z of caravanning contacts

Alde International AB
Box no. 11066
29111 Kristianstad
SWEDEN
☎ 44 4471279
Central heating systems

Alde International (UK) Ltd
Sandfield Close
Moulton Park
Northampton
ENGLAND
NN3 1AB
☎ 01604 494193
Central heating systems

AI-Ko FTF SA
Zone Industrielle de Branges
BP 99
71500 Louhans
FRANCE
☎ 03 85 76 35 00
Caravan chassis, running gear and associated products

AI-Ko Göteborg
Box 113
Trankaerrsgatan 15
42502 Hisings Kaerra/Göteborg
SWEDEN
☎ 31 570850
Caravan chassis, running gear and associated products

AI-Ko Kober BV
Diamandstraat 33
Postbus 538
7550 AM Hengelo
THE NETHERLANDS
☎ 742 559955
Caravan chassis, running gear and associated products

AI-Ko Kober GmbH
Ichenhauserstrasse 14
Postfach 61
89359 Kötz
GERMANY
☎ 8 221971
Caravan chassis, running gear and associated products

AI-Ko Kober Ltd
Queensway
Royal Leamington Spa
Warwickshire CV31 3JP
ENGLAND
☎ 01926 466500
Caravan chassis, running gear and associated products

Application des Gaz
173 Rue de Bercy
75588 Paris
Cedex 12
FRANCE
☎ 01 40 19 72 74
LPG, cylinders and appliances, lamps, heaters and camping stoves

Automobile Association
Norfolk House
Priestley Road
Basingstoke
Hampshire RG24 9NY
ENGLAND
☎ 01256 20123
Motoring organization

Automobile Club de France
6-8 Place de la Concorde
75008 Paris
FRANCE
☎ 01 43 12 43 12
Motoring organization

Automobile Club National
5 Rue Auber
75009 Paris
FRANCE
☎ 44 51 53 99
Motoring organization

Burco Maxol Ltd
Langham Street
Rosegrove
Burnley
Lancashire BB12 6AL
ENGLAND
☎ 01282 427241
LPG cookers and ovens

Calor Gas
Appleton Park
Riding Court Road
Datchet, Slough
Berkshire SL3 9JG
ENGLAND
☎ 01753 540000
LPG, cylinders, appliances and portable heaters

The Camping and Caravanning Club
Greenfields House
Westwood Way
Coventry CV4 8JH
ENGLAND
☎ 01203 694995
The oldest camping club in the world, founded in 1901. Membership of 275,000 includes tent, trailer tent, touring and motor caravan owners. Members have use of 84 sites; other services include foreign travel and technical advice.

Camping Gaz (GB) Ltd
9 Albert Street
Slough
Berkshire SL1 2BH
ENGLAND
☎ 01753 691707
LPG for caravanners

CG Sieben & Co
Basiweg 61
Postbus 333
W1000AH Amsterdam
HOLLAND
☎ 20 6139292
LPG, cylinders and appliances, lamps, heaters and camping stoves

The Caravan Club
East Grinstead House
East Grinstead
West Sussex RH19 1UA
ENGLAND
☎ 01342 326944
Club membership of 285,000 includes trailer tent, touring and motor caravan owners. With 200 club sites and 3,000 certificated locations; club services include touring guidance, towing courses, technical and holiday information.

The Caravan Club of Sweden
Filarevägen 3
70375 Oerebro
SWEDEN
☎ 19 234610
National club for caravanners

Carver & Co (Engineers) Ltd
Engine Lane
Coppice Side Industrial Estate
Brownhills
Walsall
West Midlands WS8 7ES
ENGLAND
☎ 01543 452122
Space and water heaters, and accessories

CEC Plug-in Systems
Grange Park Road
Willerby
Hull
East Yorkshire HU10 6EQ
ENGLAND
☎ 01482 652523
Electrical systems and components

Clipsal (UK) Ltd
24 Dalston Gardens
Stanmore
Middlesex HA7 1DA
ENGLAND
☎ 0181 204 9494
Electrical accessories for caravans, including sockets and switches

Datatag
95 Beverley Road
Hull
East Yorkshire HU3 1XY
ENGLAND
☎ 01482 328120
Security tagging of caravans (also motorbikes etc)

AB Electrolux
Luxbacken 1
Lilla Essingen
10545 Stockholm
SWEDEN
☎ 8 7386000
Manufacturers of caravan refrigerators and associated accessories

Electrolux Leisure Appliances
Oakley Road
Luton
Bedfordshire LU4 9QQ
ENGLAND
☎ 01582 494111
Refrigerators and accessories

Electrolux Nederland BV
Postbus 120
2400 AC Alphen ad Rijn
THE NETHERLANDS
☎ 17 2480555
Refrigerators and accessories

Electrolux SA
BP 139
60307 Senlis
FRANCE
☎ 03 44 62 20 00
Refrigerators and accessories

Elsan Ltd
Buxted
Uckfield
Sussex TN22 4LW
ENGLAND
☎ 01825 748200
Caravan toilets and chemicals

Ets Paillard SA
Zone Industrielle
BP No 501
77015 Melun-Cedex
FRANCE
☎ 0164 104880
Manufacturers of caravan brakes, hitchheads and undergear

Federation Francais de Camping et de Caravaning
78 Rue de Rivoli
75004 Paris
FRANCE
☎ 01 42 72 84 08
National club for caravanners

Fiamma SpA
c/o H Burden Ltd
Pytchley Lodge Road Industrial Estate
Kettering
Northamptonshire NN1B SJQ
ENGLAND
☎ 01536 411511
Toilets, chemicals, levelling ramps, blocks and accessories

Gimeg BV
Stijkviertel 25
3454 De Meern
THE NETHERLANDS
☎ 30 6629511
Electrical components, including 12V lights and control panels

Gimeg (UK) Ltd
8 Sedling Road
Wear East Industrial Estate
Washington
Tyne & Wear NE38 9BZ
ENGLAND
☎ 0191 415 0268
Electrical components including 12V lights and control panels

Grade (UK)
3 Central Court
Finch Close
Lenton Lane Industrial Estate
Nottingham NG7 2NN
ENGLAND
☎ 0115 986 7151
TV aerials and associated products

Halfords
The low cost telephone number 0345 626625 will switch you through to your local dealer

Hella Ltd
Wildmere Industrial Estate
Banbury
Oxfordshire OX16 7JU
ENGLAND
☎ 01295 272233
Electrical equipment and sundries for towing

Hella SA
BP No 7
11 Av Albert Einstein
93 151 Le Blanc Mesnil-Cédex
FRANCE
☎ 01 48 67 12 12
Electrical equipment and sundries for towing

Hy-Broms KB
BP Box 2041
Hammarhagsvaegen 12
14902 Nynaeshamn
SWEDEN
☎ 85 2018030
Brakes, hitchheads and undergear

Knott (UK) Ltd
Europa House
Wharf Road
Burton-on-Trent
Staffordshire DE14 1PZ
ENGLAND
☎ 01283 531541
Brakes, hitchheads and undergear

KG Knutsson AB
Hammarbacken 8
19181 Sollentuna
SWEDEN
☎ 8 92 30 00
Brakes, hitchheads and undergear

Konunklijke Nederlandsche Automobiel Club
Binckhorstlaan 115
2516 BA Den Haag
THE NETHERLANDS
☎ 70 3831612
Motoring organization

Koninklijke Nederlandse Toeristenbond
Wassenaarseweg 220
Den Haag
2596 EC
THE NETHERLANDS
☎ 70 3147147
Motoring organization

Kungl Automobil Klubben
Gyllenstiernsgatten 4
115-26 Stockholm
SWEDEN
☎ 8 6600055
Motoring organization

Lab-Craft Ltd
Bilton Road
Waterhouse Lane
Chelmsford
Essex CM1 2UP
ENGLAND
☎ 01245 859888
Lamp units, battery boxes and accessories

Maxview Aerials Ltd
Setchey
Kings Lynn
Norfolk PE33 0AT
ENGLAND
☎ 01533 810376
TV aerials, signal amplifiers and antennae

Monroe (UK) Ltd
Shipton Road
York
North Yorkshire YO3 6ZT
ENGLAND
☎ 01904 631441
Car suspension levelling systems

Motormännens (M)
Riksförbund
Sveavägen 159
104-35 Stockholm
SWEDEN
☎ 8 6903800
Motoring organization

Munster Simms Engineering
Old Belfast Road
Bangor
County Down BT19 1LT
NORTHERN IRELAND
☎ 01247 270531
Whale water supply products

Nederlandse Toeristen Kampeer Club
Ebrodreef 87
NL-3561 JM Utrecht
THE NETHERLANDS
☎ 30 618118
National Club for caravanners

Pays-Bas Nederlandse Caravan Club
Nieuwe Stationstraat 36A
NL-6711 Beede
THE NETHERLANDS
☎ 83 8019124
National club for caravanners

Polyplastic bv
Vlaarindgweg 98
3044CK Rotterdam
THE NETHERLANDS
☎ 10 4461113
Caravan windows and doors

Polyplastic UK
Europa House
Wharf Road
Burton-on-Trent
Staffordshire DE14 1PZ
ENGLAND
☎ 01283 531541
Caravan windows and doors

Primus AB
PO Box 1366
17126 Solna
SWEDEN
☎ 8 6292200
Primus gas appliances and accessories

Primus Ltd
Stevenson Way
Formby
Merseyside L37 8EQ
ENGLAND
☎ 01704 878614
Primus gas appliances and accessories

Protempo BV
Wielen en Assentechniek
Energieweg 4
Postfach 21
NL-6500 AA Nijmegen
THE NETHERLANDS
☎ 24 3773344
Brakes, hitchheads and undergear

RAC Motoring Services
PO Box 100
Bartlett Street
South Croydon
Surrey CR2 6XW
ENGLAND
Motoring organization

Remis UK
1 Manor Close
Great Harrowden
Wellingborough
Northamptonshire NN9 5AG
ENGLAND
☎ 01933 675358
Caravan window blinds

Remis SA
19 Rue de la Parcheminerie
18700 Aubigny
FRANCE
☎ 02 48 58 03 67
Caravan window blinds

Scan-terieur
30 The Metro Centre
Tolpits Lane
Watford
Hertfordshire WD1 8SB
ENGLAND
☎ 01923 800353
Seitz caravan blinds and light fittings

Sluyter BV
Postbus 1398
Celsiusbaan 2
NL – 3430 BJ Nieuwegein
THE NETHERLANDS
☎ 30 609 56 11
Electrical equipment and sundries for towing

Thetford Ltd
Unit 6
Centrovell Industrial Estate
Caldwell Road
Nuneaton
Warwickshire CV11 4UD
ENGLAND
☎ 01203 341941
Caravan toilets and chemicals

W4 Ltd
Unit B
Ford Lane Industrial Estate
Arundel
West Sussex BN18 0DF
ENGLAND
☎ 01243 553355
Towing equipment, sockets, towbar wiring kits and relay systems

Witter Towbars
18 Canal Side
Chester CH1 3LL
ENGLAND
☎ 01244 341166
Towbars and accessories

Zig Electronics Ltd
Phoenix Works
Thrupp
Stroud
ENGLAND
☎ 01453 731220
Electrical systems, control panels and battery chargers

Index

Acknowledgements

The author and publishers would like to thank the following: our main models – Graham, Ann, Michael and Kathryn Bastow – for all their cheerful help and hard work; the photographers' assistants, Hannah Grass and Ruby Wright; author's researcher, Nuala Murray; John Wickersham; Clive and Lois Edwards of Deneway Guides and Travel Ltd.

We would also like to thank:
The many companies who kindly supplied products for photography in the studio and on location. Caravans for the shoots came from the following companies: ABI (Beverley, East Yorkshire), Axxor (Les Ulis, France), Bailey (Bristol), Eriba UK (Lechlade, Gloucestershire) and Sterling (part of The Swift Group, Cottingham, East Yorkshire).

The dealers who supplied caravans were: Northam Farm (Burnham-on-Sea, Somerset), Green Pennant Caravans (Burlesdon, Nr Southampton), Golden Castle Caravans (Cheltenham Road East, Gloucester). The towcars were loaned by: IM Group (Ssangyong), Peugeot, Vauxhall, Volkswagen and Volvo.

The main photographic locations were at The Inside Park, Blandford Forum, Dorset and Northam Farm Caravan Park (Burnham-on-Sea, Somerset), who both supplied a great deal of help.

Also generous with their time and services were: The Caravan Club; The Camping and Caravanning Club; Sparkford Caravan Services (Nr Yeovil, Somerset); Davan Caravans (Weston-Super-Mare); Wimborne Caravans (Wimborne, Dorset); Halfords Superstore (Western Avenue, Yeovil, Somerset); Calor Gas (Slough and Penmill Trading Estate, Yeovil).

Props for the shoots came from:
A variety of general props:
Debenhams (Princes Street, Edinburgh); Frasers (Princes Street, Edinburgh); Argos (Edinburgh); Great Mills (Glasgow Road, Edinburgh); Asda (The Jewel, Brunstane, Edinburgh); Knowepark Caravans (Livingston, West Lothian); Lakeland Plastics (George Street, Edinburgh); Waddingtons Games; Weatherhead's of Wincanton, Somerset; Guzzini (Mitcham, Surrey); John Lewis (The Horsefair, Bristol). Clothing was supplied by Debenhams, North Cape and Racing Green.

More specific props and accessories:
Perkson Ltd (Keep-It hitchlock and wheelclamps); A H Hitchman (Aquaroll and Wastemaster water containers); Munster Simms Engineering (Whale accessories); Poplar Plastics (waste container); Carver & Co (care kit and Crystal accessories); Calor Gas; Thetford (Porta-Potti and chemicals); Varta (leisure battery); Caravan Park Electrical Services (mains cable); Energizer (torches); Hiatco (alloy step); Pyramid Plastics (Levelramp, Rise and Clamp, wheelclamps, noseweight gauge, caravan step); Al-Ko Kober (SKS 2000 stabilizer, jacks and accessories); Raydyot (towing mirrors); Kidde (fire extinguishers); Firemaster (fire blanket); E I Company (smoke alarms); BCA Leisure (towing mirrors); Teso (towing mirrors); Dimplex (electric heaters); Pifco (travel iron, kettle and hairdryer); Reed Books (road atlases and guides); Ordnance Survey (maps); Deansgate Designs (caravan alarm); International Concessionaires (Westfalia SSK stabilizer); H Burden and Co (Fiamma blocks); B Dixon Bate (Van Leveller) and towball covers; Cosmic Car Accessories (corner steady pads); Heron-Suzuki (generator); Michelin (guides); AA (travelling abroad kit); Castrol (Everyman oil); Bosal (towballs); Allibert (patio furniture); Black Knight (barbecues); Bulldog Security Products (Euroclamp and heavy duty wheelclamps); P G R Products (wheelclamps); Bradcot Awnings; The Exhaust Ejector Co (towball covers); Bird, Stevens and Co (Carapaw winter wheels); R G Trade Supplies; R D Power (battery condition monitor and charger).

Reference material to help with devising illustrations was supplied by:
ABI Caravans; Bailey Caravans; The Caravan Club; Keen Electronics; The Folding Caravan Centre (Fleurette, Esterel and Rapido caravans); Salou Awnings; Isabella Awnings; Grayston Engineering; Monroe (UK) Ltd; Ashley Banks Ltd; Ring Automotive; Hella Ltd; Freedom Caravans; Brink UK; Burstner Caravans UK; Knaus Caravans; Hobby Caravans UK; M A D Holland; Primus UK and *Practical Caravan* magazine.

Photographic credits:
Key: t top, b bottom, r right, l left
Derek Braid: main pic, 138-139; Datatag: 49br; Equibrand Tops: 49bl; The Hulton Getty Picture Collection Limited: 4t; Perkson Ltd: 49m; *Practical Caravan* magazine: 59, 98, 154, 155; A F S Rotel: 79t; Swift Group: 30.